RICH WITH
PURPOSE
INNER CIRCLE

RICH WITH
PURPOSE
INNER CIRCLE

Stone Heap Publishing
New York, NY 10023.

ISBN-13: 978-0578430447 (Custom Universal)
ISBN-10: 0578430444

MONTHLY THEMES

Self Acceptance 9
Grounding. 45
Balance 74
Focus. 103
Support 139
Transformation 168
Challenge. 197
Adventure 226
Gratitude. 255
Surrender. 291
Giving Back. 320
Flow. 349

WELCOME!

I have always had a passion for journals and blank books––it may, in fact, be my longest and costliest addiction––as well as for collecting quotes.

When I created the runaway bestselling course A YEAR TO GET RICH WITH PURPOSE for DailyOM, I began almost every lesson with at least one quote that inspired me, as well as offering journaling exercises about one's thoughts and feelings regarding the day's lesson.

Soon, more and more students began asking for this: a journal that followed the format of the course's content and had additional quotes as well.

And…drumroll…Here It Is!

Just as with the course itself you can start at any point.

(But just FYI, the best time is always NOW.)

And as with the course itself, I can't promise that by writing in this journal every day you'll be a billionaire by the year's end.

I can promise this, however: you'll become more holistically connected to both yourself AND to the world around you, living a life that truly honors yourself and serves others... and thus rewards you more richly for it.

I also guarantee if you engage in these practices, you will awaken your spirit, becoming more aware of the sacred in life's everyday moments, particularly how the Universal Life Force can demonstrate itself by flowing cash more abundantly into your bank account.

Let This Be the Year that Changes Everything...

Are you ready to begin a Guided Journey Guaranteed to

Clarify, Nourish, and Dramatically Expand Your Wealth Consciousness,

Starting Right Now?

YES! I'm ready to begin this Adventure:

_____

Please Sign & Date

This month we explore...

Self Acceptance

What does the concept of **Self Acceptance** evoke for you?

_____
_____
_____
_____

Today, I'm grateful for

1. _____
2. _____
3. _____

Today I will explore a life that's _Rich With Purpose_ by

_____
_____
_____
_____

Day 1

Over one thousand years ago Lao Tzu said
'The journey of a thousand miles begins with a single step.'
So, too, does the path towards millions of dollars.
– Edward Vilga, *The Yoga of Money Manifesto*

What thoughts and feelings does this quote inspire?

_____
_____
_____
_____

Today, I'm grateful for

1. _____
2. _____
3. _____

Today I will explore a life that's *Rich With Purpose* by

_____
_____
_____
_____

Day 2

The beginning is always today.
— Mary Wollstonecraft Shelley

What thoughts and feelings does this quote inspire?

_____
_____
_____
_____

Today, I'm grateful for

1. _____
2. _____
3. _____

Today I will explore a life that's *Rich With Purpose* by

_____
_____
_____
_____

Day 3

I am divinely guided at all times.
– Louise Haye

What thoughts and feelings does this quote inspire?

_____
_____
_____
_____

Today, I'm grateful for

1. _____
2. _____
3. _____

Today I will explore a life that's *Rich With Purpose* by

_____
_____
_____
_____

___ / ___ / ____

Day 4

We are not human beings having a spiritual experience.
We are spiritual beings having a human experience.
– Pierre Teilhard de Chardin

What thoughts and feelings does this quote inspire?

_____
_____
_____
_____

Today, I'm grateful for

1. _____
2. _____
3. _____

Today I will explore a life that's *Rich With Purpose* by

_____
_____
_____
_____

Day 5

The spiritual is the parent of the practical.
– Thomas Carlyle

What thoughts and feelings does this quote inspire?

_____

_____

_____

_____

Today, I'm grateful for

1. _____

2. _____

3. _____

Today I will explore a life that's *Rich With Purpose* by

_____

_____

_____

_____

Day 6

Eighty percent of success is showing up.
– Woody Allen

What thoughts and feelings does this quote inspire?

_____
_____
_____
_____

Today, I'm grateful for

1. _____
2. _____
3. _____

Today I will explore a life that's *Rich With Purpose* by

_____
_____
_____
_____

___ / ___ / _____   15

Day 7 • Weekly Check-in

What's come up for you this week around **Self Acceptance**?

_____

_____

_____

Have you noticed any changes in your financial life or in your
connection to purpose? Have any synchronicities occurred?

_____

_____

_____

What does your Guru Within now recommend as the wisest
path, both for your inner journey and for your action steps?

_____

_____

_____

Day 8

When you surrender to what is and so become
fully present, the past ceases to have any power.
– Eckhart Tolle, *The Power of Now*

What thoughts and feelings does this quote inspire?

_____
_____
_____
_____

Today, I'm grateful for

1. _____
2. _____
3. _____

Today I will explore a life that's *Rich With Purpose* by

_____
_____
_____
_____

Day 9

Be Here Now.
– Ram Das

What thoughts and feelings does this quote inspire?

_____
_____
_____
_____

Today, I'm grateful for

1. _____
2. _____
3. _____

Today I will explore a life that's *Rich With Purpose* by

_____
_____
_____
_____

Day 10

Feelings come and go like clouds in a windy sky.
Conscious breathing is my anchor.
– Thich Nhat Hanh

What thoughts and feelings does this quote inspire?

_____
_____
_____
_____

Today, I'm grateful for

1. _____
2. _____
3. _____

Today I will explore a life that's *Rich With Purpose* by

_____
_____
_____
_____

Day 11

Remember to breathe. It is after all, the secret of life.
— Gregory Maguire

What thoughts and feelings does this quote inspire?

_____

_____

_____

_____

Today, I'm grateful for

1. _____
2. _____
3. _____

Today I will explore a life that's *Rich With Purpose* by

_____

_____

_____

_____

Day 12

Knowing yourself is the beginning of all wisdom.
— Aristotle

What thoughts and feelings does this quote inspire?

_____
_____
_____
_____

Today, I'm grateful for

1. _____
2. _____
3. _____

Today I will explore a life that's *Rich With Purpose* by

_____
_____
_____
_____

Day 13

The Point of Power is in the Present.
– Jane Roberts

What thoughts and feelings does this quote inspire?

_____
_____
_____
_____

Today, I'm grateful for

1. _____
2. _____
3. _____

Today I will explore a life that's *Rich With Purpose* by

_____
_____
_____
_____

Day 14 • Weekly Check-in

What's come up for you this week around **Self Acceptance**?

_____

_____

_____

Have you noticed any changes in your financial life or in your connection to purpose? Have any synchronicities occurred?

_____

_____

_____

What does your Guru Within now recommend as the wisest path, both for your inner journey and for your action steps?

_____

_____

_____

Day 15

*We must be willing to get rid of the life we've planned
so as to have the life that is waiting for us.*
– Joseph Campbell

What thoughts and feelings does this quote inspire?

_____

_____

_____

_____

Today, I'm grateful for

1. _____
2. _____
3. _____

Today I will explore a life that's *Rich With Purpose* by

_____

_____

_____

_____

___ / ___ / ____

Day 16

The only way to make sense out of change is to plunge into it, move with it, and join the dance.
– Allan Watts

What thoughts and feelings does this quote inspire?

_____
_____
_____
_____

Today, I'm grateful for

1. _____
2. _____
3. _____

Today I will explore a life that's *Rich With Purpose* by

_____
_____
_____
_____

Day 17

Self Acceptance means embracing one's own uniqueness,
particularly one's injuries and vulnerabilities.
– Edward Vilga, *The Yoga of Money Manifesto*

What thoughts and feelings does this quote inspire?

_____
_____
_____
_____

Today, I'm grateful for

1. _____
2. _____
3. _____

Today I will explore a life that's *Rich With Purpose* by

_____
_____
_____
_____

Day 18

Willingness to change is a strength, even if it means plunging
part of the company into total confusion for a while.
– Jack Welch

What thoughts and feelings does this quote inspire?

_____

_____

_____

_____

Today, I'm grateful for

1. _____

2. _____

3. _____

Today I will explore a life that's *Rich With Purpose* by

_____

_____

_____

_____

Day 19

Nothing that is good can become stuck –
and if it is stuck, it can't be any good!
– Silvia Hartmann

What thoughts and feelings does this quote inspire?

_____
_____
_____
_____

Today, I'm grateful for

1. _____
2. _____
3. _____

Today I will explore a life that's *Rich With Purpose* by

_____
_____
_____
_____

Day 20

Your willingness to look at your darkness
is what empowers you to change.
– Iylana Vanzant

What thoughts and feelings does this quote inspire?

_____
_____
_____
_____

Today, I'm grateful for

1. _____
2. _____
3. _____

Today I will explore a life that's *Rich With Purpose* by

_____
_____
_____
_____

Day 21 • Weekly Check-in

What's come up for you this week around **Self Acceptance**?

_____
_____
_____

Have you noticed any changes in your financial life or in your connection to purpose? Have any synchronicities occurred?

_____
_____
_____

What does your Guru Within now recommend as the wisest path, both for your inner journey and for your action steps?

_____
_____
_____

Day 22

If we take judging ourselves and others out of our life,
we will mostly be living in paradise.
– Yogi Bhajan

What thoughts and feelings does this quote inspire?

_____

_____

_____

_____

Today, I'm grateful for

1. _____
2. _____
3. _____

Today I will explore a life that's *Rich With Purpose* by

_____

_____

_____

_____

Day 23

Definition of judgment
noun judg·ment \ ˈjəj-mənt\

the process of forming an opinion or evaluation by discerning and
comparing careful judgment of the odds

— Merriam Webster

What thoughts and feelings does this quote inspire?

_____
_____
_____
_____

Today, I'm grateful for

1. _____
2. _____
3. _____

Today I will explore a life that's *Rich With Purpose* by

_____
_____
_____
_____

Day 24

I suppose it is tempting, if the only tool you have is a hammer, to treat everything as if it were a nail.
– Abraham Maslow

What thoughts and feelings does this quote inspire?

_____

_____

_____

_____

Today, I'm grateful for

1. _____
2. _____
3. _____

Today I will explore a life that's *Rich With Purpose* by

_____

_____

_____

_____

Day 25

*If you judge people, you have
no time to love them.*
– Mother Teresa

What thoughts and feelings does this quote inspire?

_____
_____
_____
_____

Today, I'm grateful for

1. _____
2. _____
3. _____

Today I will explore a life that's *Rich With Purpose* by

_____
_____
_____
_____

Day 26

*Being angry and resentful of someone is like
letting them live rent-fre in your head.*
– George Foreman

What thoughts and feelings does this quote inspire?

_____

_____

_____

_____

Today, I'm grateful for

1. _____

2. _____

3. _____

Today I will explore a life that's *Rich With Purpose* by

_____

_____

_____

_____

Day 27

Judge nothing, you will be happy.
Forgive everything, you will be happier.
Love everything, you will be happiest.
– Sri Chinmoy

What thoughts and feelings does this quote inspire?

_____
_____
_____
_____

Today, I'm grateful for

1. _____
2. _____
3. _____

Today I will explore a life that's *Rich With Purpose* by

_____
_____
_____
_____

Day 28 • Weekly Check-in

What's come up for you this week around **Self Acceptance**?

_____

_____

_____

Have you noticed any changes in your financial life or in your
connection to purpose? Have any synchronicities occurred?

_____

_____

_____

What does your Guru Within now recommend as the wisest
path, both for your inner journey and for your action steps?

_____

_____

_____

Day 29

There is no shame in a yoga practice, nor should there be in one's financial life. You are not a bad person because you have tight hamstrings or because you have gone seriously into debt.
– Edward Vilga, *The Yoga of Money Manifesto*

What thoughts and feelings does this quote inspire?

_____

_____

_____

_____

Today, I'm grateful for

1. _____
2. _____
3. _____

Today I will explore a life that's *Rich With Purpose* by

_____

_____

_____

_____

Day 30

Shame is a soul-eating emotion.
– C.G. Jung

What thoughts and feelings does this quote inspire?

_____
_____
_____
_____

Today, I'm grateful for

1. _____
2. _____
3. _____

Today I will explore a life that's *Rich With Purpose* by

_____
_____
_____
_____

Day 31

Shame is the lie someone told you about yourself.
— Anaïs Nin

What thoughts and feelings does this quote inspire?

_____

_____

_____

_____

Today, I'm grateful for

1. _____
2. _____
3. _____

Today I will explore a life that's *Rich With Purpose* by

_____

_____

_____

_____

Day 32

You're only as sick as your secrets.
– Saying from Alcoholics Anonymous

What thoughts and feelings does this quote inspire?

_____
_____
_____
_____

Today, I'm grateful for

1. _____
2. _____
3. _____

Today I will explore a life that's *Rich With Purpose* by

_____
_____
_____
_____

Day 33

Empathy's the antidote to shame. The two most powerful words when we're in struggle: me too.
– Brene Brown

What thoughts and feelings does this quote inspire?

_____
_____
_____
_____

Today, I'm grateful for

1. _____
2. _____
3. _____

Today I will explore a life that's *Rich With Purpose* by

_____
_____
_____
_____

Day 34

The past has no power over
the present moment.
— Eckhart Tolle

What thoughts and feelings does this quote inspire?

_____
_____
_____
_____

Today, I'm grateful for

1. _____
2. _____
3. _____

Today I will explore a life that's *Rich With Purpose* by

_____
_____
_____
_____

Day 35 • Weekly Check-in

What's come up for you this week around **Self Acceptance**?

_____

_____

_____

Have you noticed any changes in your financial life or in your connection to purpose? Have any synchronicities occurred?

_____

_____

_____

What does your Guru Within now recommend as the wisest path, both for your inner journey and for your action steps?

_____

_____

_____

This month we explore...

Grounding

What does the concept of **Grounding** evoke for you?

_____
_____
_____
_____

Today, I'm grateful for

1. _____
2. _____
3. _____

Today I will explore a life that's _Rich With Purpose_ by

_____
_____
_____
_____

Day 36

*Get yourself grounded and you can navigate
even the stormiest roads in peace.*
– Steve Goodier

What thoughts and feelings does this quote inspire?

_____
_____
_____
_____

Today, I'm grateful for

1. _____
2. _____
3. _____

Today I will explore a life that's *Rich With Purpose* by

_____
_____
_____
_____

Day 37

I've looked at clouds from both sides now
From up and down and still somehow
It's cloud's illusions I recall
I really don't know clouds at all...
– Joni Mitchell

What thoughts and feelings does this quote inspire?

_____
_____
_____
_____

Today, I'm grateful for

1. _____
2. _____
3. _____

Today I will explore a life that's *Rich With Purpose* by

_____
_____
_____
_____

Day 38

Start where you are. Use what you have. Do what you can.
– Arthur Ashe

What thoughts and feelings does this quote inspire?

_____
_____
_____
_____

Today, I'm grateful for

1. _____
2. _____
3. _____

Today I will explore a life that's *Rich With Purpose* by

_____
_____
_____
_____

Day 39

*Before everything else, getting
ready is the secret of success.*
– Henry Ford

What thoughts and feelings does this quote inspire?

_____
_____
_____
_____

Today, I'm grateful for

1. _____
2. _____
3. _____

Today I will explore a life that's *Rich With Purpose* by

_____
_____
_____
_____

Day 40

Body awareness not only anchors you in the present moment,
it is a doorway out of the prison that is the ego.
– Eckhart Tolle

What thoughts and feelings does this quote inspire?

_____
_____
_____
_____

Today, I'm grateful for

1. _____
2. _____
3. _____

Today I will explore a life that's *Rich With Purpose* by

_____
_____
_____
_____

Day 41

Through awareness of the body we
remember who we really are.
– Jack Kornfield

What thoughts and feelings does this quote inspire?

_____
_____
_____
_____

Today, I'm grateful for

1. _____
2. _____
3. _____

Today I will explore a life that's *Rich With Purpose* by

_____
_____
_____
_____

Day 42 • Weekly Check-in

What's come up for you this week around **Grounding**?

_____
_____
_____

Have you noticed any changes in your financial life or in your
connection to purpose? Have any synchronicities occurred?

_____
_____
_____

What does your Guru Within now recommend as the wisest
path, both for your inner journey and for your action steps?

_____
_____
_____

Day 43

Without self-awareness we are
as babies in the cradles.
– Virginia Woolf

What thoughts and feelings does this quote inspire?

_____
_____
_____
_____

Today, I'm grateful for

1. _____
2. _____
3. _____

Today I will explore a life that's *Rich With Purpose* by

_____
_____
_____
_____

Day 44

Self-awareness is a key to self-mastery.
– Gretchen Rubin

What thoughts and feelings does this quote inspire?

_____
_____
_____
_____

Today, I'm grateful for

1. _____
2. _____
3. _____

Today I will explore a life that's *Rich With Purpose* by

_____
_____
_____
_____

Day 45

*Awareness is like the sun. When it shines
on things, they are transformed.*
– Thich Nhat Hanh

What thoughts and feelings does this quote inspire?

_____

_____

_____

_____

Today, I'm grateful for

1. _____
2. _____
3. _____

Today I will explore a life that's *Rich With Purpose* by

_____

_____

_____

_____

Day 46

*I think self-awareness is the most important
thing towards being a champion.*
– Billie Jean King

What thoughts and feelings does this quote inspire?

_____
_____
_____
_____

Today, I'm grateful for

1. _____
2. _____
3. _____

Today I will explore a life that's *Rich With Purpose* by

_____
_____
_____
_____

Day 47

The body never lies.
– Martha Graham

What thoughts and feelings does this quote inspire?

_____
_____
_____
_____

Today, I'm grateful for

1. _____
2. _____
3. _____

Today I will explore a life that's *Rich With Purpose* by

_____
_____
_____
_____

Day 48

Awareness is the greatest agent for change.
– Eckhart Tolle

What thoughts and feelings does this quote inspire?

_____
_____
_____
_____

Today, I'm grateful for

1. _____
2. _____
3. _____

Today I will explore a life that's *Rich With Purpose* by

_____
_____
_____
_____

Day 47 • Weekly Check-in

What's come up for you this week around **Grounding**?

_____

_____

_____

Have you noticed any changes in your financial life or in your connection to purpose? Have any synchronicities occurred?

_____

_____

_____

What does your Guru Within now recommend as the wisest path, both for your inner journey and for your action steps?

_____

_____

_____

Day 50

There is no ostrich pose in yoga.
– Edward Vilga

What thoughts and feelings does this quote inspire?

_____
_____
_____
_____

Today, I'm grateful for

1. _____
2. _____
3. _____

Today I will explore a life that's *Rich With Purpose* by

_____
_____
_____
_____

Day 51

It's what you whisper to yourself that has the most power.
– Robert Kiyosaki

What thoughts and feelings does this quote inspire?

_____

_____

_____

_____

Today, I'm grateful for

1. _____
2. _____
3. _____

Today I will explore a life that's *Rich With Purpose* by

_____

_____

_____

_____

Day 52

*Without physical or financial awareness, we're traveling
blind, going through the motions but essentially adrift.*
– Edward Vilga, *The Yoga of Money Manifesto*

What thoughts and feelings does this quote inspire?

_____
_____
_____
_____

Today, I'm grateful for

1. _____
2. _____
3. _____

Today I will explore a life that's *Rich With Purpose* by

_____
_____
_____
_____

Day 53

*You can avoid reality, but you cannot avoid
the consequences of avoiding reality.*
– Ayn Rand

What thoughts and feelings does this quote inspire?

_____

_____

_____

_____

Today, I'm grateful for

1. _____

2. _____

3. _____

Today I will explore a life that's *Rich With Purpose* by

_____

_____

_____

_____

Day 54

*Don't spend time beating on a wall,
hoping to transform it into a door.*
– Coco Chanel

What thoughts and feelings does this quote inspire?

_____
_____
_____
_____

Today, I'm grateful for

1. _____
2. _____
3. _____

Today I will explore a life that's *Rich With Purpose* by

_____
_____
_____
_____

Day 55

Awareness is a blissful state, not a painful one.
– Gary Zukav

What thoughts and feelings does this quote inspire?

_____
_____
_____
_____

Today, I'm grateful for

1. _____
2. _____
3. _____

Today I will explore a life that's *Rich With Purpose* by

_____
_____
_____
_____

Day 56 • Weekly Check-in

What's come up for you this week around **Grounding**?

_____
_____
_____

Have you noticed any changes in your financial life or in your connection to purpose? Have any synchronicities occurred?

_____
_____
_____

What does your Guru Within now recommend as the wisest path, both for your inner journey and for your action steps?

_____
_____
_____

___ / ___ / ____

Day 57

All human unhappiness comes from not
facing reality squarely, exactly as it is.
— Buddha

What thoughts and feelings does this quote inspire?

_____

_____

_____

_____

Today, I'm grateful for

1. _____

2. _____

3. _____

Today I will explore a life that's *Rich With Purpose* by

_____

_____

_____

_____

Day 58

Face reality as it is, not as it was
or as you wish it to be.
— Jack Welch

What thoughts and feelings does this quote inspire?

_____
_____
_____
_____

Today, I'm grateful for

1. _____
2. _____
3. _____

Today I will explore a life that's *Rich With Purpose* by

_____
_____
_____
_____

Day 59

*Avoidance is the best short-term strategy to escape conflict
and the best long-term strategy to ensure suffering.*
– Brendon Burchard

What thoughts and feelings does this quote inspire?

_____

_____

_____

_____

Today, I'm grateful for

1. _____
2. _____
3. _____

Today I will explore a life that's *Rich With Purpose* by

_____

_____

_____

_____

Day 60

You did not come to face reality,
you came to create reality.
– Abraham-Hicks

What thoughts and feelings does this quote inspire?

_____
_____
_____
_____

Today, I'm grateful for

1. _____
2. _____
3. _____

Today I will explore a life that's *Rich With Purpose* by

_____
_____
_____
_____

Day 61

When God shuts a door, He opens a window.
– attributed to everyone from Alexander Graham Bell
to Oscar Hammerstein to Helen Keller

What thoughts and feelings does this quote inspire?

_____

_____

_____

_____

Today, I'm grateful for

1. _____

2. _____

3. _____

Today I will explore a life that's *Rich With Purpose* by

_____

_____

_____

_____

Day 62

*Being realistic is the most common
path to mediocrity.*
– Will Smith

What thoughts and feelings does this quote inspire?

_____
_____
_____
_____

Today, I'm grateful for

1. _____
2. _____
3. _____

Today I will explore a life that's *Rich With Purpose* by

_____
_____
_____
_____

___ / ___ / _____

Day 61 • Weekly Check-in

What's come up for you this week around **Grounding**?

_____

_____

_____

Have you noticed any changes in your financial life or in your connection to purpose? Have any synchronicities occurred?

_____

_____

_____

What does your Guru Within now recommend as the wisest path, both for your inner journey and for your action steps?

_____

_____

_____

This month we explore...

Balance

What does the concept of **Balance** evoke for you?

_____
_____
_____
_____

Today, I'm grateful for

1. _____
2. _____
3. _____

Today I will explore a life that's _Rich With Purpose_ by

_____
_____
_____
_____

Day 64

Balance. The Ultimate Goal.
– Ricky Lankford

What thoughts and feelings does this quote inspire?

_____

_____

_____

_____

Today, I'm grateful for

1. _____
2. _____
3. _____

Today I will explore a life that's _Rich With Purpose_ by

_____

_____

_____

_____

Day 65

*If they don't have the ability to dance
with their environment, even the mightiest
oaks end up snapping like twigs.*
– Edward Vilga, *DOWNWARD DOG*

What thoughts and feelings does this quote inspire?

_____
_____
_____
_____

Today, I'm grateful for

1. _____
2. _____
3. _____

Today I will explore a life that's *Rich With Purpose* by

_____
_____
_____
_____

Day 66

*We come into this world head first and go out
feet first; in between, it is all a matter of balance.*
– Paul Boese

What thoughts and feelings does this quote inspire?

_____
_____
_____
_____

Today, I'm grateful for

1. _____
2. _____
3. _____

Today I will explore a life that's *Rich With Purpose* by

_____
_____
_____
_____

Day 67

Next to love, balance is the most important thing.
— John Wooden

What thoughts and feelings does this quote inspire?

_____

_____

_____

_____

Today, I'm grateful for

1. _____
2. _____
3. _____

Today I will explore a life that's *Rich With Purpose* by

_____

_____

_____

_____

Day 68

Happiness is not a matter of intensity but of balance and order and rhythm and harmony.
– Thomas Merton

What thoughts and feelings does this quote inspire?

_____

_____

_____

_____

Today, I'm grateful for

1. _____
2. _____
3. _____

Today I will explore a life that's *Rich With Purpose* by

_____

_____

_____

_____

Day 69

*Balance is not something you find,
it's something you create.*
– Jana Kingsford

What thoughts and feelings does this quote inspire?

_____
_____
_____
_____

Today, I'm grateful for

1. _____
2. _____
3. _____

Today I will explore a life that's *Rich With Purpose* by

_____
_____
_____
_____

Day 70 • Weekly Check-in

What's come up for you this week around **Balance**?

_____
_____
_____

Have you noticed any changes in your financial life or in your connection to purpose? Have any synchronicities occurred?

_____
_____
_____

What does your Guru Within now recommend as the wisest path, both for your inner journey and for your action steps?

_____
_____
_____

Day 71

What we all dread most is a maze with no centre.
– G. K. Chesterton

What thoughts and feelings does this quote inspire?

_____
_____
_____
_____

Today, I'm grateful for

1. _____
2. _____
3. _____

Today I will explore a life that's *Rich With Purpose* by

_____
_____
_____
_____

Day 72

Man Plans. God Laughs.
– Yiddish Proverb

What thoughts and feelings does this quote inspire?

_____

_____

_____

_____

Today, I'm grateful for

1. _____

2. _____

3. _____

Today I will explore a life that's *Rich With Purpose* by

_____

_____

_____

_____

Day 73

There is nothing so strong or safe in an
emergency of life as the simple truth.
– Charles Dickens

What thoughts and feelings does this quote inspire?

_____
_____
_____
_____

Today, I'm grateful for

1. _____
2. _____
3. _____

Today I will explore a life that's *Rich With Purpose* by

_____
_____
_____
_____

Day 74

*If you're not honest with yourself, how can
you be truly honest with anyone else?*
— Paul Williams

What thoughts and feelings does this quote inspire?

_____

_____

_____

_____

Today, I'm grateful for

1. _____

2. _____

3. _____

Today I will explore a life that's *Rich With Purpose* by

_____

_____

_____

_____

Day 75

Our necessities never equal our wants.
– Benjamin Franklin

What thoughts and feelings does this quote inspire?

_____

_____

_____

_____

Today, I'm grateful for

1. _____
2. _____
3. _____

Today I will explore a life that's *Rich With Purpose* by

_____

_____

_____

_____

Day 76

Awareness is the greatest agent for change.
– Eckhart Tolle

What thoughts and feelings does this quote inspire?

_____
_____
_____
_____

Today, I'm grateful for

1. _____
2. _____
3. _____

Today I will explore a life that's *Rich With Purpose* by

_____
_____
_____
_____

Day 77 • Weekly Check-in

What's come up for you this week around **Balance**?

_____

_____

_____

Have you noticed any changes in your financial life or in your connection to purpose? Have any synchronicities occurred?

_____

_____

_____

What does your Guru Within now recommend as the wisest path, both for your inner journey and for your action steps?

_____

_____

_____

Day 78

To believe in something, and not
to live it, is dishonest.
– Gandhi

What thoughts and feelings does this quote inspire?

_____

_____

_____

_____

Today, I'm grateful for

1. _____
2. _____
3. _____

Today I will explore a life that's *Rich With Purpose* by

_____

_____

_____

_____

Day 79

Let me be surrounded by luxury.
I can do without the necessities!
– Oscar Wilde

What thoughts and feelings does this quote inspire?

_____
_____
_____
_____

Today, I'm grateful for

1. _____
2. _____
3. _____

Today I will explore a life that's *Rich With Purpose* by

_____
_____
_____
_____

Day 80

Truly and deeply observing yourself—
and not just your ego's sales pitch— is the
best way to move beyond yourself.
– Edward Vilga

What thoughts and feelings does this quote inspire?

_____

_____

_____

_____

Today, I'm grateful for

1. _____
2. _____
3. _____

Today I will explore a life that's *Rich With Purpose* by

_____

_____

_____

_____

Day 81

We buy things we don't need,
to impress people we don't like.
– *Fight Club*, written by Chuck Palahniuk and Jim Uhls

What thoughts and feelings does this quote inspire?

_____
_____
_____
_____

Today, I'm grateful for

1. _____
2. _____
3. _____

Today I will explore a life that's *Rich With Purpose* by

_____
_____
_____
_____

Day 82

It is easy to stay present as the observer of your mind
when you are deeply rooted within your body.
– Eckhart Tolle, *The Power of Now*

What thoughts and feelings does this quote inspire?

_____

_____

_____

_____

Today, I'm grateful for

1. _____

2. _____

3. _____

Today I will explore a life that's *Rich With Purpose* by

_____

_____

_____

_____

Day 83

I love luxury.
– Coco Chanel

What thoughts and feelings does this quote inspire?

_____
_____
_____
_____

Today, I'm grateful for

1. _____
2. _____
3. _____

Today I will explore a life that's *Rich With Purpose* by

_____
_____
_____
_____

Day 82 • Weekly Check-in

What's come up for you this week around **Balance**?

_____

_____

_____

Have you noticed any changes in your financial life or in your connection to purpose? Have any synchronicities occurred?

_____

_____

_____

What does your Guru Within now recommend as the wisest path, both for your inner journey and for your action steps?

_____

_____

_____

Day 85

Trust your instincts. Intuition doesn't lie.
– Oprah Winfrey

What thoughts and feelings does this quote inspire?

_____

_____

_____

_____

Today, I'm grateful for

1. _____
2. _____
3. _____

Today I will explore a life that's *Rich With Purpose* by

_____

_____

_____

_____

Day 86

We have all a better guide in ourselves, if we
would attend to it, than any other person can be.
– Jane Austin

What thoughts and feelings does this quote inspire?

_____
_____
_____
_____

Today, I'm grateful for

1. _____
2. _____
3. _____

Today I will explore a life that's *Rich With Purpose* by

_____
_____
_____
_____

Day 87

There is a voice that doesn't use words.
Listen!
– Rumi

What thoughts and feelings does this quote inspire?

_____
_____
_____
_____

Today, I'm grateful for

1. _____
2. _____
3. _____

Today I will explore a life that's *Rich With Purpose* by

_____
_____
_____
_____

Day 88

Anyone can plot a course with a map or compass;
but without a sense of who you are, you will
never know if you're already home.
– Shannon L. Alder

What thoughts and feelings does this quote inspire?

_____
_____
_____
_____

Today, I'm grateful for

1. _____
2. _____
3. _____

Today I will explore a life that's *Rich With Purpose* by

_____
_____
_____
_____

Day 89

The primary wisdom is intuition.
– Emerson

What thoughts and feelings does this quote inspire?

_____
_____
_____
_____

Today, I'm grateful for

1. _____
2. _____
3. _____

Today I will explore a life that's *Rich With Purpose* by

_____
_____
_____
_____

Day 90

*Every time you don't follow your inner guidance, you feel a
loss of energy, loss of power, a sense of spiritual deadness.*
– Shakti Gawain

What thoughts and feelings does this quote inspire?

_____
_____
_____
_____

Today, I'm grateful for

1. _____
2. _____
3. _____

Today I will explore a life that's *Rich With Purpose* by

_____
_____
_____
_____

Day 91 • Weekly Check-in

What's come up for you this week around **Balance**?

_____
_____
_____

Have you noticed any changes in your financial life or in your
connection to purpose? Have any synchronicities occurred?

_____
_____
_____

What does your Guru Within now recommend as the wisest
path, both for your inner journey and for your action steps?

_____
_____
_____

This month we explore...

Focus

What does the concept of **Focus** evoke for you?

_____
_____
_____
_____

Today, I'm grateful for

1. _____
2. _____
3. _____

Today I will explore a life that's *Rich With Purpose* by

_____
_____
_____
_____

Day 92

It's time to dive deeper into creating financial goals, one that authentically inspire us. You've dared to dream—and dared to Dream Big. Now it's time to begin to narrow and focus those dreams if you want them to really come true.
– Edward Vilga

What thoughts and feelings does this quote inspire?

_____
_____
_____
_____

Today, I'm grateful for

1. _____
2. _____
3. _____

Today I will explore a life that's *Rich With Purpose* by

_____
_____
_____
_____

Day 93

All successful people, men and women, are big dreamers. They imagine what their future could be, ideal in every respect, and then they work every day toward their distant vision, that goal or purpose.
— Brian Tracy

What thoughts and feelings does this quote inspire?

_____

_____

_____

_____

Today, I'm grateful for

1. _____
2. _____
3. _____

Today I will explore a life that's *Rich With Purpose* by

_____

_____

_____

_____

Day 94

Cherish your visions and your dreams, as they are the children of your soul, the blueprints of your ultimate achievements.
– Napoleon Hill

What thoughts and feelings does this quote inspire?

_____
_____
_____
_____

Today, I'm grateful for

1. _____
2. _____
3. _____

Today I will explore a life that's *Rich With Purpose* by

_____
_____
_____
_____

Day 95

*To accomplish great things, we must not only act,
but also dream; not only plan, but also believe.*
– Anatole France

What thoughts and feelings does this quote inspire?

_____
_____
_____
_____

Today, I'm grateful for

1. _____
2. _____
3. _____

Today I will explore a life that's *Rich With Purpose* by

_____
_____
_____
_____

Day 96

The future belongs to those who believe
in the beauty of their dreams.
— Eleanor Roosevelt

What thoughts and feelings does this quote inspire?

_____
_____
_____
_____

Today, I'm grateful for

1. _____
2. _____
3. _____

Today I will explore a life that's *Rich With Purpose* by

_____
_____
_____
_____

Day 97

If a little dreaming is dangerous, the cure for it is not to dream less but to dream more, to dream all the time.
– Marcel Proust

What thoughts and feelings does this quote inspire?

_____
_____
_____
_____

Today, I'm grateful for

1. _____
2. _____
3. _____

Today I will explore a life that's *Rich With Purpose* by

_____
_____
_____
_____

Day 98 • Weekly Check-in

What's come up for you this week around **Focus**?

_____

_____

_____

Have you noticed any changes in your financial life or in your connection to purpose? Have any synchronicities occurred?

_____

_____

_____

What does your Guru Within now recommend as the wisest path, both for your inner journey and for your action steps?

_____

_____

_____

Day 99

*But little by little,
as you left their voice behind,
the stars began to burn
through the sheets of clouds,
and there was a new voice
which you slowly
recognized as your own...*
– Mary Oliver, *The Journey*

What thoughts and feelings does this quote inspire?

_____
_____
_____
_____

Today, I'm grateful for

1. _____
2. _____
3. _____

Today I will explore a life that's *Rich With Purpose* by

_____
_____
_____
_____

Day 100

*To be yourself in a world that is constantly
trying to make you something else is
the greatest accomplishment.*

– Emerson

What thoughts and feelings does this quote inspire?

_____

_____

_____

_____

Today, I'm grateful for

1. _____

2. _____

3. _____

Today I will explore a life that's *Rich With Purpose* by

_____

_____

_____

_____

Day 101

*No one man can, for any considerable time, wear one
face to himself, and another to the multitude, without
finally getting bewildered as to which is the true one.*
– Nathaniel Hawthorne

What thoughts and feelings does this quote inspire?

_____

_____

_____

_____

Today, I'm grateful for

1. _____
2. _____
3. _____

Today I will explore a life that's *Rich With Purpose* by

_____

_____

_____

_____

Day 102

*Man, sometimes it takes you a long
time to sound like yourself.*
– Miles Davis

What thoughts and feelings does this quote inspire?

_____

_____

_____

_____

Today, I'm grateful for

1. _____
2. _____
3. _____

Today I will explore a life that's *Rich With Purpose* by

_____

_____

_____

_____

Day 103

*The privilege of a lifetime is to
become who you truly are.*
– C.G. Jung

What thoughts and feelings does this quote inspire?

_____

_____

_____

_____

Today, I'm grateful for

1. _____
2. _____
3. _____

Today I will explore a life that's *Rich With Purpose* by

_____

_____

_____

_____

Day 104

This above all:
To thine own self be true,
And it must follow, as the night the day,
Thou canst not then be false to any man.
— *Hamlet* by William Shakespeare

What thoughts and feelings does this quote inspire?

_____
_____
_____
_____

Today, I'm grateful for

1. _____
2. _____
3. _____

Today I will explore a life that's *Rich With Purpose* by

_____
_____
_____
_____

Day 105 • Weekly Check-in

What's come up for you this week around **Focus**?

_____

_____

_____

Have you noticed any changes in your financial life or in your connection to purpose? Have any synchronicities occurred?

_____

_____

_____

What does your Guru Within now recommend as the wisest path, both for your inner journey and for your action steps?

_____

_____

_____

Day 106

You've dared to dream—and dared to Dream Big.
Now it's time to begin to narrow and focus those dreams.
— Edward Vilga

What thoughts and feelings does this quote inspire?

_____
_____
_____
_____

Today, I'm grateful for

1. _____
2. _____
3. _____

Today I will explore a life that's *Rich With Purpose* by

_____
_____
_____
_____

Day 107

All my life, I've always wanted to be somebody,
but I see now I should have been more specific.
– Lily Tomlin and Jane Wagner

What thoughts and feelings does this quote inspire?

_____
_____
_____
_____

Today, I'm grateful for

1. _____
2. _____
3. _____

Today I will explore a life that's *Rich With Purpose* by

_____
_____
_____
_____

Day 108

If you can't measure it, you can't improve it.
— Peter Drucker

What thoughts and feelings does this quote inspire?

_____
_____
_____
_____

Today, I'm grateful for

1. _____
2. _____
3. _____

Today I will explore a life that's *Rich With Purpose* by

_____
_____
_____
_____

Day 109

You can do anything, but not everything.
– David Allen

What thoughts and feelings does this quote inspire?

_____
_____
_____
_____

Today, I'm grateful for

1. _____
2. _____
3. _____

Today I will explore a life that's *Rich With Purpose* by

_____
_____
_____
_____

Day 110

Focusing is about saying No.
— Steve Jobs

What thoughts and feelings does this quote inspire?

_____
_____
_____
_____

Today, I'm grateful for

1. _____
2. _____
3. _____

Today I will explore a life that's *Rich With Purpose* by

_____
_____
_____
_____

Day 111

Money is not real. It is a conscious
agreement on measuring value.
– John Ralston Saul

What thoughts and feelings does this quote inspire?

_____
_____
_____
_____

Today, I'm grateful for

1. _____
2. _____
3. _____

Today I will explore a life that's *Rich With Purpose* by

_____
_____
_____
_____

Day 112 • Weekly Check-in

What's come up for you this week around **Focus**?

_____

_____

_____

Have you noticed any changes in your financial life or in your
connection to purpose? Have any synchronicities occurred?

_____

_____

_____

What does your Guru Within now recommend as the wisest
path, both for your inner journey and for your action steps?

_____

_____

_____

Day 113

Lack of direction, not lack of time, is the problem.
We all have twenty-four hour days.
– Zig Ziglar

What thoughts and feelings does this quote inspire?

_____
_____
_____
_____

Today, I'm grateful for

1. _____
2. _____
3. _____

Today I will explore a life that's *Rich With Purpose* by

_____
_____
_____
_____

Day 114

A goal is a dream with a deadline.
– Napoleon Hill

What thoughts and feelings does this quote inspire?

_____
_____
_____
_____

Today, I'm grateful for

1. _____
2. _____
3. _____

Today I will explore a life that's *Rich With Purpose* by

_____
_____
_____
_____

Day 115

One must work with time and not against it.
– Ursula K. Le Guin

What thoughts and feelings does this quote inspire?

_____
_____
_____
_____

Today, I'm grateful for

1. _____
2. _____
3. _____

Today I will explore a life that's *Rich With Purpose* by

_____
_____
_____
_____

Day 116

When you are courting a nice girl an hour seems like a second. When you sit on a red-hot cinder a second seems like an hour. That's relativity.
– Albert Einstein

What thoughts and feelings does this quote inspire?

_____

_____

_____

_____

Today, I'm grateful for

1. _____

2. _____

3. _____

Today I will explore a life that's *Rich With Purpose* by

_____

_____

_____

_____

Day 117

Always focus on the front windshield
and not the review mirror.
– Colin Powell

What thoughts and feelings does this quote inspire?

_____
_____
_____
_____

Today, I'm grateful for

1. _____
2. _____
3. _____

Today I will explore a life that's *Rich With Purpose* by

_____
_____
_____
_____

Day 118

'I love deadlines. I like the whooshing sound they make as they fly by.'
– Douglas Adams

What thoughts and feelings does this quote inspire?

_____
_____
_____
_____

Today, I'm grateful for

1. _____
2. _____
3. _____

Today I will explore a life that's *Rich With Purpose* by

_____
_____
_____
_____

Day 119 • Weekly Check-in

What's come up for you this week around **Focus**?

_____
_____
_____

Have you noticed any changes in your financial life or in your connection to purpose? Have any synchronicities occurred?

_____
_____
_____

What does your Guru Within now recommend as the wisest path, both for your inner journey and for your action steps?

_____
_____
_____

Day 120

I am always doing that which I cannot do,
in order that I may learn how to do it.
— Pablo Picasso

What thoughts and feelings does this quote inspire?

_____
_____
_____
_____

Today, I'm grateful for

1. _____
2. _____
3. _____

Today I will explore a life that's *Rich With Purpose* by

_____
_____
_____
_____

Day 121

We have found that by reaching for what appears to be the impossible, we often actually do the impossible; and even when we don't quite make it, we inevitably wind up doing much better than we would have done.
— Jack Welch

What thoughts and feelings does this quote inspire?

_____

_____

_____

_____

Today, I'm grateful for

1. _____
2. _____
3. _____

Today I will explore a life that's *Rich With Purpose* by

_____

_____

_____

_____

Day 122

*The greater danger for most of us isn't
that our aim is too high and we miss it,
but that it is too low and we reach it.*
– Michelangelo

What thoughts and feelings does this quote inspire?

_____
_____
_____
_____

Today, I'm grateful for

1. _____
2. _____
3. _____

Today I will explore a life that's *Rich With Purpose* by

_____
_____
_____
_____

Day 123

*Always do your best. What you plant
now, you will harvest later.*
– Og Mandino

What thoughts and feelings does this quote inspire?

_____
_____
_____
_____

Today, I'm grateful for

1. _____
2. _____
3. _____

Today I will explore a life that's *Rich With Purpose* by

_____
_____
_____
_____

Day 124

Rome wasn't built in a day.
– Proverb

What thoughts and feelings does this quote inspire?

_____
_____
_____
_____

Today, I'm grateful for

1. _____
2. _____
3. _____

Today I will explore a life that's *Rich With Purpose* by

_____
_____
_____
_____

Day 125

Ah, but a man's reach should exceed
his grasp, Or what's a heaven for?
– Robert Browning

What thoughts and feelings does this quote inspire?

_____
_____
_____
_____

Today, I'm grateful for

1. _____
2. _____
3. _____

Today I will explore a life that's *Rich With Purpose* by

_____
_____
_____
_____

Day 126 • Weekly Check-in

What's come up for you this week around **Focus**?

_____
_____
_____

Have you noticed any changes in your financial life or in your connection to purpose? Have any synchronicities occurred?

_____
_____
_____

What does your Guru Within now recommend as the wisest path, both for your inner journey and for your action steps?

_____
_____
_____

___ / ___ / ____

This month we explore...

Support

What does the concept of **Support** evoke for you?

_____
_____
_____
_____

Today, I'm grateful for

1. _____
2. _____
3. _____

Today I will explore a life that's _Rich With Purpose_ by

_____
_____
_____
_____

Day 127

We don't accomplish anything in this world alone.
– Sandra Day O'Connor

What thoughts and feelings does this quote inspire?

_____
_____
_____
_____

Today, I'm grateful for

1. _____
2. _____
3. _____

Today I will explore a life that's *Rich With Purpose* by

_____
_____
_____
_____

Day 128

No one can do it alone.
– Arnold Schwarzenegger

What thoughts and feelings does this quote inspire?

_____

_____

_____

_____

Today, I'm grateful for

1. _____

2. _____

3. _____

Today I will explore a life that's *Rich With Purpose* by

_____

_____

_____

_____

Day 129

Set your life on fire. Seek those who fan your flames.
— Rumi

What thoughts and feelings does this quote inspire?

_____
_____
_____
_____

Today, I'm grateful for

1. _____
2. _____
3. _____

Today I will explore a life that's *Rich With Purpose* by

_____
_____
_____
_____

Day 130

Support is not 'one size fits all.'
– Edward Vilga

What thoughts and feelings does this quote inspire?

_____

_____

_____

_____

Today, I'm grateful for

1. _____
2. _____
3. _____

Today I will explore a life that's *Rich With Purpose* by

_____

_____

_____

_____

Day 131

To keep a lamp burning we have
to keep putting oil in it.
– Mother Theresa

What thoughts and feelings does this quote inspire?

_____
_____
_____
_____

Today, I'm grateful for

1. _____
2. _____
3. _____

Today I will explore a life that's *Rich With Purpose* by

_____
_____
_____
_____

Day 132

Make a habit of two things: to help;
or at least to do no harm.
– Hippocrates

What thoughts and feelings does this quote inspire?

_____

_____

_____

_____

Today, I'm grateful for

1. _____
2. _____
3. _____

Today I will explore a life that's *Rich With Purpose* by

_____

_____

_____

_____

Day 133 • Weekly Check-in

What's come up for you this week around **Support**?

_____

_____

_____

Have you noticed any changes in your financial life or in your
connection to purpose? Have any synchronicities occurred?

_____

_____

_____

What does your Guru Within now recommend as the wisest
path, both for your inner journey and for your action steps?

_____

_____

_____

Day 134

Our prime purpose in this life is to help others.
And if you can't help them, at least don't hurt them.
– Dalai Lama

What thoughts and feelings does this quote inspire?

_____
_____
_____
_____

Today, I'm grateful for

1. _____
2. _____
3. _____

Today I will explore a life that's *Rich With Purpose* by

_____
_____
_____
_____

Day 135

Be strong, be fearless, be beautiful.
And believe that anything is possible when you
have the right people there to support you.
– Misty Copeland

What thoughts and feelings does this quote inspire?

_____
_____
_____
_____

Today, I'm grateful for

1. _____
2. _____
3. _____

Today I will explore a life that's *Rich With Purpose* by

_____
_____
_____
_____

Day 136

*Whenever we're afraid to ask for something,
it's usually because we're really afraid of
plunging down the rabbit hole of self-worth.*
– Edward Vilga

What thoughts and feelings does this quote inspire?

_____

_____

_____

_____

Today, I'm grateful for

1. _____

2. _____

3. _____

Today I will explore a life that's *Rich With Purpose* by

_____

_____

_____

_____

Day 137

*No act of kindness, no matter
how small, is ever wasted.*

– Aesop

What thoughts and feelings does this quote inspire?

_____
_____
_____
_____

Today, I'm grateful for

1. _____
2. _____
3. _____

Today I will explore a life that's *Rich With Purpose* by

_____
_____
_____
_____

Day 138

When we ask for anything, we're almost always asking for help, in some form.
– Amanda Palmer

What thoughts and feelings does this quote inspire?

_____

_____

_____

_____

Today, I'm grateful for

1. _____
2. _____
3. _____

Today I will explore a life that's *Rich With Purpose* by

_____

_____

_____

_____

Day 139

*The only mistake you can make
is not asking for help.*
– Sandeep Jauhar

What thoughts and feelings does this quote inspire?

_____
_____
_____
_____

Today, I'm grateful for

1. _____
2. _____
3. _____

Today I will explore a life that's *Rich With Purpose* by

_____
_____
_____
_____

Day 140 • Weekly Check-in

What's come up for you this week around **Support**?

_____

_____

_____

Have you noticed any changes in your financial life or in your connection to purpose? Have any synchronicities occurred?

_____

_____

_____

What does your Guru Within now recommend as the wisest path, both for your inner journey and for your action steps?

_____

_____

_____

Day 141

The purpose of life is not to be happy. It is to be useful,
to be honorable, to be compassionate, to have it make
some difference that you have lived and lived well.
– Ralph Waldo Emerson

What thoughts and feelings does this quote inspire?

_____

_____

_____

_____

Today, I'm grateful for

1. _____
2. _____
3. _____

Today I will explore a life that's *Rich With Purpose* by

_____

_____

_____

_____

Day 142

Cultivate:

1 : to prepare or prepare and use for the raising of crops; Some fields are cultivated while others lie fallow.
2 : to foster the growth of; cultivate vegetables, cultivate coffee
  : to improve by labor, care, or study
3 : further, encourage; cultivate the arts
4 : to seek the society of, make friends with
  – Merriam Webster

What thoughts and feelings does this quote inspire?

_____
_____
_____
_____

Today, I'm grateful for

1. _____
2. _____
3. _____

Today I will explore a life that's *Rich With Purpose* by

_____
_____
_____
_____

Day 143

*No one is useless in this world who
lightens the burdens of another.*
– Charles Dickens

What thoughts and feelings does this quote inspire?

_____
_____
_____
_____

Today, I'm grateful for

1. _____
2. _____
3. _____

Today I will explore a life that's *Rich With Purpose* by

_____
_____
_____
_____

Day 144

When we give cheerfully and accept gratefully, everyone is blessed.
– Maya Angelou

What thoughts and feelings does this quote inspire?

_____
_____
_____
_____

Today, I'm grateful for

1. _____
2. _____
3. _____

Today I will explore a life that's *Rich With Purpose* by

_____
_____
_____
_____

Day 145

Love all.
Trust a few.
Do wrong to none.
— Proverb

What thoughts and feelings does this quote inspire?

_____
_____
_____
_____

Today, I'm grateful for

1. _____
2. _____
3. _____

Today I will explore a life that's *Rich With Purpose* by

_____
_____
_____
_____

Day 146

When we seek to discover the best in others,
we somehow bring out the best in ourselves.
– William Arthur Ward

What thoughts and feelings does this quote inspire?

_____
_____
_____
_____

Today, I'm grateful for

1. _____
2. _____
3. _____

Today I will explore a life that's *Rich With Purpose* by

_____
_____
_____
_____

Day 147 • Weekly Check-in

What's come up for you this week around **Support**?

_____

_____

_____

Have you noticed any changes in your financial life or in your connection to purpose? Have any synchronicities occurred?

_____

_____

_____

What does your Guru Within now recommend as the wisest path, both for your inner journey and for your action steps?

_____

_____

_____

Day 148

We only have what we give.
– Isabel Allende

What thoughts and feelings does this quote inspire?

_____
_____
_____
_____

Today, I'm grateful for

1. _____
2. _____
3. _____

Today I will explore a life that's *Rich With Purpose* by

_____
_____
_____
_____

Day 149

Motivation is what gets you started.
Habit is what keeps you going.
– Jim Ryun

What thoughts and feelings does this quote inspire?

_____

_____

_____

_____

Today, I'm grateful for

1. _____
2. _____
3. _____

Today I will explore a life that's *Rich With Purpose* by

_____

_____

_____

_____

Day 150

We are what we repeatedly do.
Excellence, then, is not an act, but a habit.
– Aristotle

What thoughts and feelings does this quote inspire?

_____
_____
_____
_____

Today, I'm grateful for

1. _____
2. _____
3. _____

Today I will explore a life that's *Rich With Purpose* by

_____
_____
_____
_____

Day 151

We become what we repeatedly do.
– Sean Covey

What thoughts and feelings does this quote inspire?

_____
_____
_____
_____

Today, I'm grateful for

1. _____
2. _____
3. _____

Today I will explore a life that's *Rich With Purpose* by

_____
_____
_____
_____

Day 152

The first hour of the morning is the rudder of the day.
– Henry Ward Beecher

What thoughts and feelings does this quote inspire?

_____

_____

_____

_____

Today, I'm grateful for

1. _____

2. _____

3. _____

Today I will explore a life that's *Rich With Purpose* by

_____

_____

_____

_____

Day 153

People say that motivation doesn't last.
Well, neither does bathing.
That's why we recommend it daily.
– Zig Ziglar

What thoughts and feelings does this quote inspire?

_____
_____
_____
_____

Today, I'm grateful for

1. _____
2. _____
3. _____

Today I will explore a life that's *Rich With Purpose* by

_____
_____
_____
_____

Day 154 • Weekly Check-in

What's come up for you this week around **Support**?

_____

_____

_____

Have you noticed any changes in your financial life or in your
connection to purpose? Have any synchronicities occurred?

_____

_____

_____

What does your Guru Within now recommend as the wisest
path, both for your inner journey and for your action steps?

_____

_____

_____

This month we explore...

Transformation

What does the concept of **Transformation** evoke for you?

_____

_____

_____

_____

Today, I'm grateful for

1. _____
2. _____
3. _____

Today I will explore a life that's _Rich With Purpose_ by

_____

_____

_____

_____

Day 155

Your Upper Limit is False.
— Edward Vilga

What thoughts and feelings does this quote inspire?

_____

_____

_____

_____

Today, I'm grateful for

1. _____

2. _____

3. _____

Today I will explore a life that's *Rich With Purpose* by

_____

_____

_____

_____

Day 156

The Upper Limit Problem is the only problem we need to solve.
– Gay Hendricks, *The Big Leap*

What thoughts and feelings does this quote inspire?

_____

_____

_____

_____

Today, I'm grateful for

1. _____

2. _____

3. _____

Today I will explore a life that's *Rich With Purpose* by

_____

_____

_____

_____

Day 157

Embrace the glorious mess that you are.
– Elizabeth Gilbert

What thoughts and feelings does this quote inspire?

_____

_____

_____

_____

Today, I'm grateful for

1. _____

2. _____

3. _____

Today I will explore a life that's *Rich With Purpose* by

_____

_____

_____

_____

Day 158

Any fool can make a rule
And any fool will mind it.
– Henry David Thoreau

What thoughts and feelings does this quote inspire?

_____
_____
_____
_____

Today, I'm grateful for

1. _____
2. _____
3. _____

Today I will explore a life that's *Rich With Purpose* by

_____
_____
_____
_____

Day 159

Mo Money, Mo Problems.
– Notorious B.I.G.

What thoughts and feelings does this quote inspire?

_____
_____
_____
_____

Today, I'm grateful for

1. _____
2. _____
3. _____

Today I will explore a life that's *Rich With Purpose* by

_____
_____
_____
_____

Day 160

Our deepest fear is not that we are inadequate.
Our deepest fear is that we are powerful beyond measure.
It is our light, not our darkness that most frightens us.
— Marianne Williamson, *A Return To Love*

What thoughts and feelings does this quote inspire?

_____

_____

_____

_____

Today, I'm grateful for

1. _____
2. _____
3. _____

Today I will explore a life that's *Rich With Purpose* by

_____

_____

_____

_____

Day 161 • Weekly Check-in

What's come up for you this week around **Transformation**?

_____

_____

_____

Have you noticed any changes in your financial life or in your connection to purpose? Have any synchronicities occurred?

_____

_____

_____

What does your Guru Within now recommend as the wisest path, both for your inner journey and for your action steps?

_____

_____

_____

Day 162

Since they reveal the deepest parts of ourselves, if we listen wisely, sometimes even our worst fears can offer us great gifts.
– Edward Vilga

What thoughts and feelings does this quote inspire?

_____

_____

_____

_____

Today, I'm grateful for

1. _____
2. _____
3. _____

Today I will explore a life that's *Rich With Purpose* by

_____

_____

_____

_____

Day 163

Fears are nothing more than a state of mind.
– Napoleon Hill, *Think & Grow Rich*

What thoughts and feelings does this quote inspire?

_____

_____

_____

_____

Today, I'm grateful for

1. _____
2. _____
3. _____

Today I will explore a life that's *Rich With Purpose* by

_____

_____

_____

_____

Day 164

Irrational fear feeds on itself and grows. You must deny it.
– Dean Koontz, *Brother Odd*

What thoughts and feelings does this quote inspire?

_____
_____
_____
_____

Today, I'm grateful for

1. _____
2. _____
3. _____

Today I will explore a life that's *Rich With Purpose* by

_____
_____
_____
_____

Day 165

Fear: False Evidence Appearing Real.
– Well-Known Saying

What thoughts and feelings does this quote inspire?

_____
_____
_____
_____

Today, I'm grateful for

1. _____
2. _____
3. _____

Today I will explore a life that's *Rich With Purpose* by

_____
_____
_____
_____

Day 166

It's important to keep remembering that we are not just a single cell Grand Total on an Excel spreadsheet.
– Edward Vilga, *The Yoga of Money Manifesto*

What thoughts and feelings does this quote inspire?

_____

_____

_____

_____

Today, I'm grateful for

1. _____
2. _____
3. _____

Today I will explore a life that's *Rich With Purpose* by

_____

_____

_____

_____

Day 167

The oldest and strongest emotion of mankind is fear, and the oldest and strongest kind of fear is fear of the unknown.
– H. P. Lovecraft

What thoughts and feelings does this quote inspire?

_____
_____
_____
_____

Today, I'm grateful for

1. _____
2. _____
3. _____

Today I will explore a life that's *Rich With Purpose* by

_____
_____
_____
_____

Day 168 • Weekly Check-in

What's come up for you this week around **Transformation**?

_____

_____

_____

Have you noticed any changes in your financial life or in your connection to purpose? Have any synchronicities occurred?

_____

_____

_____

What does your Guru Within now recommend as the wisest path, both for your inner journey and for your action steps?

_____

_____

_____

Day 169

A story has no beginning or end: arbitrarily one chooses that moment of experience from which to look back or from which to look ahead.
– Graham Greene

What thoughts and feelings does this quote inspire?

_____

_____

_____

_____

Today, I'm grateful for

1. _____
2. _____
3. _____

Today I will explore a life that's *Rich With Purpose* by

_____

_____

_____

_____

Day 170

Inside each of us is a natural-born storyteller, waiting to be released.
— Robin Moore

What thoughts and feelings does this quote inspire?

_____
_____
_____
_____

Today, I'm grateful for

1. _____
2. _____
3. _____

Today I will explore a life that's *Rich With Purpose* by

_____
_____
_____
_____

Day 171

*You're never going to kill storytelling because
it's built into the human plan. We come with it.*
— Margaret Atwood

What thoughts and feelings does this quote inspire?

_____
_____
_____
_____

Today, I'm grateful for

1. _____
2. _____
3. _____

Today I will explore a life that's *Rich With Purpose* by

_____
_____
_____
_____

Day 172

*Stories create community, enable us to
see through the eyes of other people,
and open us to the claims of others.*
— Peter Forbes

What thoughts and feelings does this quote inspire?

_____
_____
_____
_____

Today, I'm grateful for

1. _____
2. _____
3. _____

Today I will explore a life that's *Rich With Purpose* by

_____
_____
_____
_____

Day 173

Sometimes reality is too complex.
Stories give it form.
– Jean Luc Goddard

What thoughts and feelings does this quote inspire?

_____
_____
_____
_____

Today, I'm grateful for

1. _____
2. _____
3. _____

Today I will explore a life that's *Rich With Purpose* by

_____
_____
_____
_____

Day 174

Story is a yearning meeting an obstacle.
– Robert Olen Butler

What thoughts and feelings does this quote inspire?

_____
_____
_____
_____

Today, I'm grateful for

1. _____
2. _____
3. _____

Today I will explore a life that's *Rich With Purpose* by

_____
_____
_____
_____

Day 175 • Weekly Check-in

What's come up for you this week around **Transformation**?

_____

_____

_____

Have you noticed any changes in your financial life or in your
connection to purpose? Have any synchronicities occurred?

_____

_____

_____

What does your Guru Within now recommend as the wisest
path, both for your inner journey and for your action steps?

_____

_____

_____

Day 176

If you're going to have a story, have a big story, or none at all.
– Joseph Campbell

What thoughts and feelings does this quote inspire?

_____

_____

_____

_____

Today, I'm grateful for

1. _____

2. _____

3. _____

Today I will explore a life that's *Rich With Purpose* by

_____

_____

_____

_____

Day 177

Tragedy plus time equals comedy.
– Steve Allen

What thoughts and feelings does this quote inspire?

_____
_____
_____
_____

Today, I'm grateful for

1. _____
2. _____
3. _____

Today I will explore a life that's *Rich With Purpose* by

_____
_____
_____
_____

Day 178

The unexamined life is not worth living.
– Plato

What thoughts and feelings does this quote inspire?

_____

_____

_____

_____

Today, I'm grateful for

1. _____
2. _____
3. _____

Today I will explore a life that's *Rich With Purpose* by

_____

_____

_____

_____

Day 179

There is no greater agony than bearing
an untold story inside you.
– Maya Angelou

What thoughts and feelings does this quote inspire?

_____
_____
_____
_____

Today, I'm grateful for

1. _____
2. _____
3. _____

Today I will explore a life that's *Rich With Purpose* by

_____
_____
_____
_____

Day 180

*Real generosity towards the future
lies in giving all to the present.*
– Albert Camus

What thoughts and feelings does this quote inspire?

_____
_____
_____
_____

Today, I'm grateful for

1. _____
2. _____
3. _____

Today I will explore a life that's *Rich With Purpose* by

_____
_____
_____
_____

Day 181

*The only difference between the saint and the sinner is that
every saint has a past, and every sinner has a future.*
– Oscar Wilde

What thoughts and feelings does this quote inspire?

_____
_____
_____
_____

Today, I'm grateful for

1. _____
2. _____
3. _____

Today I will explore a life that's *Rich With Purpose* by

_____
_____
_____
_____

Day 182 • Weekly Check-in

What's come up for you this week around **Transformation**?

_____

_____

_____

Have you noticed any changes in your financial life or in your connection to purpose? Have any synchronicities occurred?

_____

_____

_____

What does your Guru Within now recommend as the wisest path, both for your inner journey and for your action steps?

_____

_____

_____

This month we explore...

Challenge

What does the concept of **Challenge** evoke for you?

_____
_____
_____
_____

Today, I'm grateful for

1. _____
2. _____
3. _____

Today I will explore a life that's _Rich With Purpose_ by

_____
_____
_____
_____

Day 183

Everything's a story—You are a story—I am a story.
— Frances Hodgson Burnett

What thoughts and feelings does this quote inspire?

_____
_____
_____
_____

Today, I'm grateful for

1. _____
2. _____
3. _____

Today I will explore a life that's *Rich With Purpose* by

_____
_____
_____
_____

Day 184

We are the stories we tell ourselves.
– Joan Didion

What thoughts and feelings does this quote inspire?

_____
_____
_____
_____

Today, I'm grateful for

1. _____
2. _____
3. _____

Today I will explore a life that's *Rich With Purpose* by

_____
_____
_____
_____

Day 185

The past is just a story we tell ourselves.
– Spike Jonze, *Her*

What thoughts and feelings does this quote inspire?

_____
_____
_____
_____

Today, I'm grateful for

1. _____
2. _____
3. _____

Today I will explore a life that's *Rich With Purpose* by

_____
_____
_____
_____

Day 186

We become the stories we tell ourselves.
– Michael Cunningham

What thoughts and feelings does this quote inspire?

_____
_____
_____
_____

Today, I'm grateful for

1. _____
2. _____
3. _____

Today I will explore a life that's *Rich With Purpose* by

_____
_____
_____
_____

Day 187

Who are we but the stories we tell ourselves,
about ourselves, and believe?
– Scott Turow, *Ordinary Heroes*

What thoughts and feelings does this quote inspire?

_____
_____
_____
_____

Today, I'm grateful for

1. _____
2. _____
3. _____

Today I will explore a life that's *Rich With Purpose* by

_____
_____
_____
_____

Day 188

When you understand that what you're telling is just
a story. It isn't happening anymore. When you realize
the story you're telling is just words, when you can
just crumble up and throw your past in the trashcan,
then we'll figure out who you're going to be.
– Chuck Palahniuk, *Invisible Monsters*

What thoughts and feelings does this quote inspire?

_____
_____
_____
_____

Today, I'm grateful for

1. _____
2. _____
3. _____

Today I will explore a life that's *Rich With Purpose* by

_____
_____
_____
_____

Day 189 • Weekly Check-in

What's come up for you this week around **Challenge**?

_____

_____

_____

Have you noticed any changes in your financial life or in your
connection to purpose? Have any synchronicities occurred?

_____

_____

_____

What does your Guru Within now recommend as the wisest
path, both for your inner journey and for your action steps?

_____

_____

_____

Day 190

Ask yourself who you really are.
Be prepared to be astonished at the answer.
– Edward Vilga

What thoughts and feelings does this quote inspire?

_____
_____
_____
_____

Today, I'm grateful for

1. _____
2. _____
3. _____

Today I will explore a life that's *Rich With Purpose* by

_____
_____
_____
_____

Day 191

Drink from the well of yourself and begin again.
– Charles Bukowski

What thoughts and feelings does this quote inspire?

_____

_____

_____

_____

Today, I'm grateful for

1. _____
2. _____
3. _____

Today I will explore a life that's *Rich With Purpose* by

_____

_____

_____

_____

Day 192

*Always be a first rate version of yourself and
not a second rate version of someone else.*
– Judy Garland

What thoughts and feelings does this quote inspire?

_____

_____

_____

_____

Today, I'm grateful for

1. _____
2. _____
3. _____

Today I will explore a life that's *Rich With Purpose* by

_____

_____

_____

_____

Day 193

Let yourself be drawn by the stronger
pull of that which you truly love.
– Rumi

What thoughts and feelings does this quote inspire?

_____

_____

_____

_____

Today, I'm grateful for

1. _____
2. _____
3. _____

Today I will explore a life that's *Rich With Purpose* by

_____

_____

_____

_____

Day 194

Follow your inner moonlight;
don't hide the madness.
– Allen Ginsberg

What thoughts and feelings does this quote inspire?

_____
_____
_____
_____

Today, I'm grateful for

1. _____
2. _____
3. _____

Today I will explore a life that's *Rich With Purpose* by

_____
_____
_____
_____

Day 195

Be yourself; everyone else is already taken.
— Oscar Wilde

What thoughts and feelings does this quote inspire?

_____
_____
_____
_____

Today, I'm grateful for

1. _____
2. _____
3. _____

Today I will explore a life that's *Rich With Purpose* by

_____
_____
_____
_____

Day 196 • Weekly Check-in

What's come up for you this week around **Challenge**?

_____

_____

_____

Have you noticed any changes in your financial life or in your connection to purpose? Have any synchronicities occurred?

_____

_____

_____

What does your Guru Within now recommend as the wisest path, both for your inner journey and for your action steps?

_____

_____

_____

Day 197

Tell the story that's been growing in your heart...
– Jennifer Weiner

What thoughts and feelings does this quote inspire?

_____
_____
_____
_____

Today, I'm grateful for

1. _____
2. _____
3. _____

Today I will explore a life that's *Rich With Purpose* by

_____
_____
_____
_____

Day 198

Things in life have no real beginning,
though our stories about them always do.
– Colum McCann

What thoughts and feelings does this quote inspire?

_____
_____
_____
_____

Today, I'm grateful for

1. _____
2. _____
3. _____

Today I will explore a life that's *Rich With Purpose* by

_____
_____
_____
_____

Day 199

*The road to success and the road to failure
are almost exactly the same.*
– Colin R. Davis

What thoughts and feelings does this quote inspire?

_____
_____
_____
_____

Today, I'm grateful for

1. _____
2. _____
3. _____

Today I will explore a life that's *Rich With Purpose* by

_____
_____
_____
_____

Day 200

Opportunities don't happen. You create them.
– Chris Grosser

What thoughts and feelings does this quote inspire?

_____
_____
_____
_____

Today, I'm grateful for

1. _____
2. _____
3. _____

Today I will explore a life that's *Rich With Purpose* by

_____
_____
_____
_____

Day 201

Dreaming may seem like an unaffordable indulgence, yet if we are to have the life we really want—and the money to pay for it!—we must first reconnect with our true desires and aspirations.
– Edward Vilga, *The Yoga of Money Manifesto*

What thoughts and feelings does this quote inspire?

_____
_____
_____
_____

Today, I'm grateful for

1. _____
2. _____
3. _____

Today I will explore a life that's *Rich With Purpose* by

_____
_____
_____
_____

Day 202

*I'm a great believer in luck, and I find the
harder I work the more I have of it.*
– Coleman Cox

What thoughts and feelings does this quote inspire?

_____
_____
_____
_____

Today, I'm grateful for

1. _____
2. _____
3. _____

Today I will explore a life that's *Rich With Purpose* by

_____
_____
_____
_____

Day 203 • Weekly Check-in

What's come up for you this week around **Challenge**?

_____
_____
_____

Have you noticed any changes in your financial life or in your
connection to purpose? Have any synchronicities occurred?

_____
_____
_____

What does your Guru Within now recommend as the wisest
path, both for your inner journey and for your action steps?

_____
_____
_____

Day 204

*Don't let the fear of losing be greater
than the excitement of winning.*
– Robert Kiyosaki

What thoughts and feelings does this quote inspire?

_____

_____

_____

_____

Today, I'm grateful for

1. _____
2. _____
3. _____

Today I will explore a life that's *Rich With Purpose* by

_____

_____

_____

_____

Day 205

You are the Hero of your own Story.
– Joseph Campbell

What thoughts and feelings does this quote inspire?

_____
_____
_____
_____

Today, I'm grateful for

1. _____
2. _____
3. _____

Today I will explore a life that's *Rich With Purpose* by

_____
_____
_____
_____

Day 206

The way to get started is to quit talking and begin doing.
– Walt Disney

What thoughts and feelings does this quote inspire?

_____
_____
_____
_____

Today, I'm grateful for

1. _____
2. _____
3. _____

Today I will explore a life that's *Rich With Purpose* by

_____
_____
_____
_____

Day 207

I shall be telling this with a sigh
Somewhere ages and ages hence:
Two roads diverged in a wood, and I—
I took the one less traveled by,
And that has made all the difference.
– Robert Frost

What thoughts and feelings does this quote inspire?

_____
_____
_____
_____

Today, I'm grateful for

1. _____
2. _____
3. _____

Today I will explore a life that's *Rich With Purpose* by

_____
_____
_____
_____

Day 208

Until one is committed, there is hesitancy, the chance to draw
back, always ineffectiveness. Concerning all acts of initiative
(and creation), there is one elementary truth, the ignorance of
which kills countless ideas and splendid plans: that the moment
one definitely commits oneself, then Providence moves too.
– attributed often to Goethe, but probably William Hutchison Murray

What thoughts and feelings does this quote inspire?

_____

_____

_____

_____

Today, I'm grateful for

1. _____

2. _____

3. _____

Today I will explore a life that's *Rich With Purpose* by

_____

_____

_____

_____

Day 209

*If you are not the hero of your own story,
then you're missing the whole point of your humanity.*
– Steve Maraboli

What thoughts and feelings does this quote inspire?

_____
_____
_____
_____

Today, I'm grateful for

1. _____
2. _____
3. _____

Today I will explore a life that's *Rich With Purpose* by

_____
_____
_____
_____

Day 210 • Weekly Check-in

What's come up for you this week around **Challenge**?

_____

_____

_____

Have you noticed any changes in your financial life or in your
connection to purpose? Have any synchronicities occurred?

_____

_____

_____

What does your Guru Within now recommend as the wisest
path, both for your inner journey and for your action steps?

_____

_____

_____

This month we explore...

Adventure

What does the concept of **Adventure** evoke for you?

_____

_____

_____

_____

Today, I'm grateful for

1. _____

2. _____

3. _____

Today I will explore a life that's _Rich With Purpose_ by

_____

_____

_____

_____

Day 211

Playing safe is very risky.
– Seth Godin

What thoughts and feelings does this quote inspire?

_____
_____
_____
_____

Today, I'm grateful for

1. _____
2. _____
3. _____

Today I will explore a life that's *Rich With Purpose* by

_____
_____
_____
_____

Day 212

*From a certain point onward there is no longer any
turning back. That is the point that must be reached.*
— Seneca

What thoughts and feelings does this quote inspire?

_____
_____
_____
_____

Today, I'm grateful for

1. _____
2. _____
3. _____

Today I will explore a life that's *Rich With Purpose* by

_____
_____
_____
_____

Day 213

Life is either a daring adventure or nothing at all.
— Helen Keller

What thoughts and feelings does this quote inspire?

_____
_____
_____
_____

Today, I'm grateful for

1. _____
2. _____
3. _____

Today I will explore a life that's *Rich With Purpose* by

_____
_____
_____
_____

Day 214

Travel far enough, you meet yourself.
– David Mitchell

What thoughts and feelings does this quote inspire?

_____

_____

_____

_____

Today, I'm grateful for

1. _____
2. _____
3. _____

Today I will explore a life that's *Rich With Purpose* by

_____

_____

_____

Day 215

*Only those who risk going too far can
possibly find out how far they can go.*
– T.S. Elliot

What thoughts and feelings does this quote inspire?

_____
_____
_____
_____

Today, I'm grateful for

1. _____
2. _____
3. _____

Today I will explore a life that's *Rich With Purpose* by

_____
_____
_____
_____

Day 216

Adventure is worthwhile in itself.
– Amelia Earhart

What thoughts and feelings does this quote inspire?

_____
_____
_____
_____

Today, I'm grateful for

1. _____
2. _____
3. _____

Today I will explore a life that's *Rich With Purpose* by

_____
_____
_____
_____

Day 217 • Weekly Check-in

What's come up for you this week around **Adventure**?

_____

_____

_____

Have you noticed any changes in your financial life or in your connection to purpose? Have any synchronicities occurred?

_____

_____

_____

What does your Guru Within now recommend as the wisest path, both for your inner journey and for your action steps?

_____

_____

_____

Day 218

One way to get the most out of life is
to look upon it as an adventure.
– William Feather

What thoughts and feelings does this quote inspire?

_____
_____
_____
_____

Today, I'm grateful for

1. _____
2. _____
3. _____

Today I will explore a life that's *Rich With Purpose* by

_____
_____
_____
_____

Day 219

If you're willing to see things from a fresh perspective,
almost everything in life can be regarded as an adventure.
– Edward Vilga

What thoughts and feelings does this quote inspire?

_____
_____
_____
_____

Today, I'm grateful for

1. _____
2. _____
3. _____

Today I will explore a life that's *Rich With Purpose* by

_____
_____
_____
_____

Day 220

I think I'm quite ready for another adventure!
– J.R.R. Tolkien, *Lord of the Rings: The Return of the King*

What thoughts and feelings does this quote inspire?

_____
_____
_____
_____

Today, I'm grateful for

1. _____
2. _____
3. _____

Today I will explore a life that's *Rich With Purpose* by

_____
_____
_____
_____

Day 221

We are spirits in the material world.
– Sting, *The Police*

What thoughts and feelings does this quote inspire?

_____
_____
_____
_____

Today, I'm grateful for

1. _____
2. _____
3. _____

Today I will explore a life that's *Rich With Purpose* by

_____
_____
_____
_____

Day 222

The hero returns to the world of common day and must accept it as real.
– Joseph Campbell

What thoughts and feelings does this quote inspire?

_____
_____
_____
_____

Today, I'm grateful for

1. _____
2. _____
3. _____

Today I will explore a life that's *Rich With Purpose* by

_____
_____
_____
_____

Day 223

This embodiment of spirit in the physical is one of great challenges of human existence. Fortunately, this contrast is what allows us the freedom to dance.
— Edward Vilga

What thoughts and feelings does this quote inspire?

_____
_____
_____
_____

Today, I'm grateful for

1. _____
2. _____
3. _____

Today I will explore a life that's *Rich With Purpose* by

_____
_____
_____
_____

Day 224 • Weekly Check-in

What's come up for you this week around **Adventure**?

_____

_____

_____

Have you noticed any changes in your financial life or in your connection to purpose? Have any synchronicities occurred?

_____

_____

_____

What does your Guru Within now recommend as the wisest path, both for your inner journey and for your action steps?

_____

_____

_____

Day 225

I hope you see things that startle you. I hope you feel things you never felt before. I hope you meet people with a different point of view. I hope you live a life you're proud of. If you find that you're not, I hope you have the strength to start all over again.
— Eric Roth, *The Curious Case of Benjamin Button*

What thoughts and feelings does this quote inspire?

_____

_____

_____

_____

Today, I'm grateful for

1. _____
2. _____
3. _____

Today I will explore a life that's *Rich With Purpose* by

_____

_____

_____

_____

Day 226

A ship is safe in harbor, but that's
not what ships are built for.
– John A. Shedd

What thoughts and feelings does this quote inspire?

_____
_____
_____
_____

Today, I'm grateful for

1. _____
2. _____
3. _____

Today I will explore a life that's *Rich With Purpose* by

_____
_____
_____
_____

Day 227

In the Chinese language, the word "crisis" is composed of two characters, one representing danger and the other, opportunity.
– John F. Kennedy

What thoughts and feelings does this quote inspire?

_____
_____
_____
_____

Today, I'm grateful for

1. _____
2. _____
3. _____

Today I will explore a life that's *Rich With Purpose* by

_____
_____
_____
_____

Day 228

Always remember, it's simply not an adventure worth telling if there aren't any dragons.
– Sarah Ban Breathnach

What thoughts and feelings does this quote inspire?

_____
_____
_____
_____

Today, I'm grateful for

1. _____
2. _____
3. _____

Today I will explore a life that's *Rich With Purpose* by

_____
_____
_____
_____

Day 229

Believe me! The secret of reaping the greatest fruitfulness
and the greatest enjoyment from life is to live dangerously!
– Friedrich Nietzsche

What thoughts and feelings does this quote inspire?

_____

_____

_____

_____

Today, I'm grateful for

1. _____
2. _____
3. _____

Today I will explore a life that's *Rich With Purpose* by

_____

_____

_____

_____

Day 230

If things seem under control,
you are just not going fast enough.
– Mario Andretti

What thoughts and feelings does this quote inspire?

_____
_____
_____
_____

Today, I'm grateful for

1. _____
2. _____
3. _____

Today I will explore a life that's *Rich With Purpose* by

_____
_____
_____
_____

Day 231 • Weekly Check-in

What's come up for you this week around **Adventure**?

_____

_____

_____

Have you noticed any changes in your financial life or in your
connection to purpose? Have any synchronicities occurred?

_____

_____

_____

What does your Guru Within now recommend as the wisest
path, both for your inner journey and for your action steps?

_____

_____

_____

Day 232

*Move out of your comfort zone. You can only
grow if you are willing to feel awkward and
uncomfortable when you try something new.*
– Brian Tracy

What thoughts and feelings does this quote inspire?

_____
_____
_____
_____

Today, I'm grateful for

1. _____
2. _____
3. _____

Today I will explore a life that's *Rich With Purpose* by

_____
_____
_____
_____

Day 233

And the day came when the wish to
remain tight in a bud was more painful
than the risk it took to blossom.
– Anais Nin

What thoughts and feelings does this quote inspire?

_____
_____
_____
_____

Today, I'm grateful for

1. _____
2. _____
3. _____

Today I will explore a life that's *Rich With Purpose* by

_____
_____
_____
_____

Day 234

Security is mostly a superstition. It does not exist in nature, nor do the children of men as a whole experience it. Avoiding danger is no safer in the long run than outright exposure.
– Helen Keller

What thoughts and feelings does this quote inspire?

_____
_____
_____
_____

Today, I'm grateful for

1. _____
2. _____
3. _____

Today I will explore a life that's *Rich With Purpose* by

_____
_____
_____
_____

Day 235

*The only question in life is whether
or not you are going to answer a
hearty 'YES!' to your adventure.*
– Joseph Campbell

What thoughts and feelings does this quote inspire?

_____

_____

_____

_____

Today, I'm grateful for

1. _____
2. _____
3. _____

Today I will explore a life that's *Rich With Purpose* by

_____

_____

_____

_____

Day 236

Adventure isn't hanging on a rope off the side of a mountain. Adventure is an attitude that we must apply to the day to day obstacles in life.
– John Amatt

What thoughts and feelings does this quote inspire?

_____
_____
_____
_____

Today, I'm grateful for

1. _____
2. _____
3. _____

Today I will explore a life that's *Rich With Purpose* by

_____
_____
_____
_____

Day 237

Never forget that life can only be nobly inspired and rightly lived if you take it bravely and gallantly, as a splendid adventure in which you are setting out into an unknown country, to face many a danger, to meet many a joy, to find many a comrade, to win and lose many a battle.
– Annie Besant

What thoughts and feelings does this quote inspire?

_____

_____

_____

_____

Today, I'm grateful for

1. _____
2. _____
3. _____

Today I will explore a life that's *Rich With Purpose* by

_____

_____

_____

_____

Day 238 • Weekly Check-in

What's come up for you this week around **Adventure**?

_____
_____
_____

Have you noticed any changes in your financial life or in your
connection to purpose? Have any synchronicities occurred?

_____
_____
_____

What does your Guru Within now recommend as the wisest
path, both for your inner journey and for your action steps?

_____
_____
_____

This month we explore...

Gratitude

What does the concept of **Gratitude** evoke for you?

_____
_____
_____
_____

Today, I'm grateful for

1. _____
2. _____
3. _____

Today I will explore a life that's *Rich With Purpose* by

_____
_____
_____
_____

Day 239

Gratitude is not only the greatest of virtues,
but the parent of all the others.
— Cicero

What thoughts and feelings does this quote inspire?

_____
_____
_____
_____

Today, I'm grateful for

1. _____
2. _____
3. _____

Today I will explore a life that's *Rich With Purpose* by

_____
_____
_____
_____

Day 240

You, yourself, as much as anyone in the entire Universe, deserve your own love and affection.
– Buddha

What thoughts and feelings does this quote inspire?

_____

_____

_____

_____

Today, I'm grateful for

1. _____

2. _____

3. _____

Today I will explore a life that's *Rich With Purpose* by

_____

_____

_____

_____

Day 241

Bless yourself with exquisite self-care.
— SARK

What thoughts and feelings does this quote inspire?

_____
_____
_____
_____

Today, I'm grateful for

1. _____
2. _____
3. _____

Today I will explore a life that's *Rich With Purpose* by

_____
_____
_____
_____

Day 242

I found the greatest love of all inside of me.
– sung by Whitney Houston, song by Michael Masser and Linda Creed

What thoughts and feelings does this quote inspire?

_____
_____
_____
_____

Today, I'm grateful for

1. _____
2. _____
3. _____

Today I will explore a life that's *Rich With Purpose* by

_____
_____
_____
_____

Day 243

If you don't love yourself, how in the
hell you gonna love somebody else?
– RuPaul

What thoughts and feelings does this quote inspire?

_____

_____

_____

_____

Today, I'm grateful for

1. _____
2. _____
3. _____

Today I will explore a life that's *Rich With Purpose* by

_____

_____

_____

_____

Day 244

*The single most important person you
should never take for granted is you.*
– Edward Vilga

What thoughts and feelings does this quote inspire?

_____
_____
_____
_____

Today, I'm grateful for

1. _____
2. _____
3. _____

Today I will explore a life that's *Rich With Purpose* by

_____
_____
_____
_____

Day 245 • Weekly Check-in

What's come up for you this week around **Gratitude**?

_____

_____

_____

Have you noticed any changes in your financial life or in your
connection to purpose? Have any synchronicities occurred?

_____

_____

_____

What does your Guru Within now recommend as the wisest
path, both for your inner journey and for your action steps?

_____

_____

_____

Day 246

You'd be so easy to love.
– Cole Porter

What thoughts and feelings does this quote inspire?

_____
_____
_____
_____

Today, I'm grateful for

1. _____
2. _____
3. _____

Today I will explore a life that's *Rich With Purpose* by

_____
_____
_____
_____

Day 247

Thank you for being a friend
Traveled down a road and back again
Your heart is true, you're a pal and a confidant.
— Andrew Gold, *Golden Girls theme song*

What thoughts and feelings does this quote inspire?

_____
_____
_____
_____

Today, I'm grateful for

1. _____
2. _____
3. _____

Today I will explore a life that's *Rich With Purpose* by

_____
_____
_____
_____

Day 248

Recognize the other person is you.
– Yogi Bhajan

What thoughts and feelings does this quote inspire?

_____
_____
_____
_____

Today, I'm grateful for

1. _____
2. _____
3. _____

Today I will explore a life that's *Rich With Purpose* by

_____
_____
_____
_____

Day 249

The heart has its reasons which reason knows not.
– Blaire Pascal

What thoughts and feelings does this quote inspire?

_____
_____
_____
_____

Today, I'm grateful for

1. _____
2. _____
3. _____

Today I will explore a life that's *Rich With Purpose* by

_____
_____
_____
_____

Day 250

*I love you because the entire universe
conspired to help me find you.*
Paulo Coelho, *The Alchemist*

What thoughts and feelings does this quote inspire?

_____

_____

_____

_____

Today, I'm grateful for

1. _____
2. _____
3. _____

Today I will explore a life that's *Rich With Purpose* by

_____

_____

_____

_____

Day 251

You are the finest, loveliest, tenderest, and most beautiful person
I have ever known and even that is an understatement.
– F. Scott Fitzgerald

What thoughts and feelings does this quote inspire?

_____
_____
_____
_____

Today, I'm grateful for

1. _____
2. _____
3. _____

Today I will explore a life that's *Rich With Purpose* by

_____
_____
_____
_____

Day 252 • Weekly Check-in

What's come up for you this week around **Gratitude**?

_____

_____

_____

Have you noticed any changes in your financial life or in your connection to purpose? Have any synchronicities occurred?

_____

_____

_____

What does your Guru Within now recommend as the wisest path, both for your inner journey and for your action steps?

_____

_____

_____

Day 253

*It's truly amazing how so much of our lives is
filled to the brim with the miraculous and yet how
often the vast substance of it we take for granted.*
– Edward Vilga

What thoughts and feelings does this quote inspire?

_____
_____
_____
_____

Today, I'm grateful for

1. _____
2. _____
3. _____

Today I will explore a life that's *Rich With Purpose* by

_____
_____
_____
_____

Day 254

There's a story behind everything. How a picture got on a wall. How a scar got on your face. Sometimes the stories are simple, and sometimes they are hard and heartbreaking.
– Mitch Albom, *For One More Day*

What thoughts and feelings does this quote inspire?

_____
_____
_____
_____

Today, I'm grateful for

1. _____
2. _____
3. _____

Today I will explore a life that's *Rich With Purpose* by

_____
_____
_____
_____

Day 255

"Got my hair, Got my head
Got my brains, Got my ears
Got my eyes, Got my nose
Got my mouth, I got my smile
I got my tongue, Got my chin
Got my neck, Got my boobs
Got my heart, Got my soul
Got my back, I got my sex

I got my arms, Got my hands
Got my fingers, Got my legs
Got my feet, Got my toes
Got my liver, Got my blood
I've got life!"

– "I Got Life" from the Broadway musical *Hair*, lyrics by James Rado and Gerome Ragni

What thoughts and feelings does this quote inspire?

_____
_____
_____
_____

Today, I'm grateful for

1. _____
2. _____
3. _____

Today I will explore a life that's *Rich With Purpose* by

_____
_____
_____
_____

Day 256

Lose your mind and come to your senses.
– Fritz Perls

What thoughts and feelings does this quote inspire?

_____
_____
_____
_____

Today, I'm grateful for

1. _____
2. _____
3. _____

Today I will explore a life that's *Rich With Purpose* by

_____
_____
_____
_____

Day 257

All of us were born into an economic
system we did not create.
– Edward Vilga

What thoughts and feelings does this quote inspire?

_____
_____
_____
_____

Today, I'm grateful for

1. _____
2. _____
3. _____

Today I will explore a life that's *Rich With Purpose* by

_____
_____
_____
_____

Day 258

I'm Nobody! Who are you?
Are you – Nobody – too?
– Emily Dickinson

What thoughts and feelings does this quote inspire?

_____

_____

_____

_____

Today, I'm grateful for

1. _____
2. _____
3. _____

Today I will explore a life that's *Rich With Purpose* by

_____

_____

_____

_____

Day 259 • Weekly Check-in

What's come up for you this week around **Gratitude**?

_____
_____
_____

Have you noticed any changes in your financial life or in your connection to purpose? Have any synchronicities occurred?

_____
_____
_____

What does your Guru Within now recommend as the wisest path, both for your inner journey and for your action steps?

_____
_____
_____

Day 260

Do I not destroy my enemies when
I make them my friends?
– Abraham Lincoln

What thoughts and feelings does this quote inspire?

_____
_____
_____
_____

Today, I'm grateful for

1. _____
2. _____
3. _____

Today I will explore a life that's *Rich With Purpose* by

_____
_____
_____
_____

Day 261

If you aren't in over your head,
how do you know how tall you are?
– T.S. Eliot

What thoughts and feelings does this quote inspire?

_____
_____
_____
_____

Today, I'm grateful for

1. _____
2. _____
3. _____

Today I will explore a life that's *Rich With Purpose* by

_____
_____
_____
_____

Day 262

A smooth sea never made a skillful sailor.
– Proverb

What thoughts and feelings does this quote inspire?

_____
_____
_____
_____

Today, I'm grateful for

1. _____
2. _____
3. _____

Today I will explore a life that's *Rich With Purpose* by

_____
_____
_____
_____

Day 263

Pay attention to the timeless core of your being.
— Deepak Chopra

What thoughts and feelings does this quote inspire?

_____
_____
_____
_____

Today, I'm grateful for

1. _____
2. _____
3. _____

Today I will explore a life that's *Rich With Purpose* by

_____
_____
_____
_____

Day 264

Life is too short for fake butter or fake people.
— Karen Salmansohn

What thoughts and feelings does this quote inspire?

_____
_____
_____
_____

Today, I'm grateful for

1. _____
2. _____
3. _____

Today I will explore a life that's *Rich With Purpose* by

_____
_____
_____
_____

Day 265

If it doesn't challenge you, it doesn't change you.
– Fred DeVito

What thoughts and feelings does this quote inspire?

_____
_____
_____
_____

Today, I'm grateful for

1. _____
2. _____
3. _____

Today I will explore a life that's *Rich With Purpose* by

_____
_____
_____
_____

Day 266 • Weekly Check-in

What's come up for you this week around **Gratitude**?

_____

_____

_____

Have you noticed any changes in your financial life or in your connection to purpose? Have any synchronicities occurred?

_____

_____

_____

What does your Guru Within now recommend as the wisest path, both for your inner journey and for your action steps?

_____

_____

_____

Day 267

*Living in a state of gratitude is
the gateway to grace.*
– Ariana Huffington

What thoughts and feelings does this quote inspire?

_____
_____
_____
_____

Today, I'm grateful for

1. _____
2. _____
3. _____

Today I will explore a life that's *Rich With Purpose* by

_____
_____
_____
_____

Day 268

The Great Way is not difficult for
those who have no preferences.
– Zen Proverb

What thoughts and feelings does this quote inspire?

_____
_____
_____
_____

Today, I'm grateful for

1. _____
2. _____
3. _____

Today I will explore a life that's *Rich With Purpose* by

_____
_____
_____
_____

Day 269

Be content with what you have:
rejoice in the way things are.
When you realize there is nothing lacking,
the whole world belongs to you.
– Lao-Tzu

What thoughts and feelings does this quote inspire?

_____
_____
_____
_____

Today, I'm grateful for

1. _____
2. _____
3. _____

Today I will explore a life that's *Rich With Purpose* by

_____
_____
_____
_____

Day 270

We could never have guessed
We were already blessed
where we are...
– James Taylor

What thoughts and feelings does this quote inspire?

_____

_____

_____

_____

Today, I'm grateful for

1. _____

2. _____

3. _____

Today I will explore a life that's *Rich With Purpose* by

_____

_____

_____

_____

Day 271

*Wear gratitude like a cloak and it will
feed every corner of your life.*
– Rumi

What thoughts and feelings does this quote inspire?

_____
_____
_____
_____

Today, I'm grateful for

1. _____
2. _____
3. _____

Today I will explore a life that's *Rich With Purpose* by

_____
_____
_____
_____

Day 272

*Allow the wonders to be woven in, along with
all the challenging, crunchy, less than wonderfull
moments. This puts you into the "marvelous messy
middle" of your life, where all the juicy stuff lives.
It's in this middle place that all the miracles occur.*
– SARK

What thoughts and feelings does this quote inspire?

_____
_____
_____
_____

Today, I'm grateful for

1. _____
2. _____
3. _____

Today I will explore a life that's *Rich With Purpose* by

_____
_____
_____
_____

Day 273 • Weekly Check-in

What's come up for you this week around **Gratitude**?

_____

_____

_____

Have you noticed any changes in your financial life or in your
connection to purpose? Have any synchronicities occurred?

_____

_____

_____

What does your Guru Within now recommend as the wisest
path, both for your inner journey and for your action steps?

_____

_____

_____

This month we explore...

Surrender

What does the concept of **Surrender** evoke for you?

_____
_____
_____
_____

Today, I'm grateful for

1. _____
2. _____
3. _____

Today I will explore a life that's _Rich With Purpose_ by

_____
_____
_____
_____

Day 274

In the process of letting go you will lose many things from the past but you will find yourself.
– Deepak Chopra

What thoughts and feelings does this quote inspire?

_____

_____

_____

_____

Today, I'm grateful for

1. _____
2. _____
3. _____

Today I will explore a life that's *Rich With Purpose* by

_____

_____

_____

_____

Day 275

What you resist persists.
– Carl Jung

What thoughts and feelings does this quote inspire?

_____
_____
_____
_____

Today, I'm grateful for

1. _____
2. _____
3. _____

Today I will explore a life that's *Rich With Purpose* by

_____
_____
_____
_____

Day 276

Forgiveness is the magnet which draws your
endless good. It wipes clean the slate of the
past to let you receive in the present.
– Catherine Ponder

What thoughts and feelings does this quote inspire?

_____
_____
_____
_____

Today, I'm grateful for

1. _____
2. _____
3. _____

Today I will explore a life that's *Rich With Purpose* by

_____
_____
_____
_____

Day 277

Forgiveness is the fragrance that the violet
sheds on the heel that has crushed it.
– Mark Twain

What thoughts and feelings does this quote inspire?

_____
_____
_____
_____

Today, I'm grateful for

1. _____
2. _____
3. _____

Today I will explore a life that's *Rich With Purpose* by

_____
_____
_____
_____

Day 278

*I realized that my battle to survive this war
would have to be fought inside of me.*
– Immaculée Ilibagiza, *Left to Tell: Discovering
God Amidst the Rwandan Holocaust*

What thoughts and feelings does this quote inspire?

_____
_____
_____
_____

Today, I'm grateful for

1. _____
2. _____
3. _____

Today I will explore a life that's *Rich With Purpose* by

_____
_____
_____
_____

Day 279

Always forgive your enemies;
nothing annoys them so much.
– Oscar Wilde

What thoughts and feelings does this quote inspire?

_____
_____
_____
_____

Today, I'm grateful for

1. _____
2. _____
3. _____

Today I will explore a life that's *Rich With Purpose* by

_____
_____
_____
_____

Day 280 • Weekly Check-in

What's come up for you this week around **Gratitude**?

_____
_____
_____

Have you noticed any changes in your financial life or in your
connection to purpose? Have any synchronicities occurred?

_____
_____
_____

What does your Guru Within now recommend as the wisest
path, both for your inner journey and for your action steps?

_____
_____
_____

Day 281

Worry's greatest trick is that it masquerades as being helpful when it very rarely serves that purpose.
– Edward Vilga

What thoughts and feelings does this quote inspire?

_____

_____

_____

_____

Today, I'm grateful for

1. _____
2. _____
3. _____

Today I will explore a life that's *Rich With Purpose* by

_____

_____

_____

_____

Day 282

Worry is like throwing kerosene on a flame.
– Suki James

What thoughts and feelings does this quote inspire?

_____
_____
_____
_____

Today, I'm grateful for

1. _____
2. _____
3. _____

Today I will explore a life that's *Rich With Purpose* by

_____
_____
_____
_____

Day 283

When I look back on all these worries,
I remember the story of the old man who said
on his deathbed that he had had a lot of trouble
in his life, most of which had never happened.
– Winston Churchill (also ascribed to Mark Twain and others).

What thoughts and feelings does this quote inspire?

_____
_____
_____
_____

Today, I'm grateful for

1. _____
2. _____
3. _____

Today I will explore a life that's *Rich With Purpose* by

_____
_____
_____
_____

Day 284

Worry never robs tomorrow of its
sorrow, it only saps today of its joy.
– Leo F. Buscaglia

What thoughts and feelings does this quote inspire?

_____
_____
_____
_____

Today, I'm grateful for

1. _____
2. _____
3. _____

Today I will explore a life that's *Rich With Purpose* by

_____
_____
_____
_____

Day 285

*The trouble with most people is that they want
to know the way and the channels beforehand.
They want to tell Supreme Intelligence just how
their prayers should be answered. They do
not trust the wisdom and ingenuity of God.*
– Florence Scovel Shinn, The Power of the Spoken Word

What thoughts and feelings does this quote inspire?

_____
_____
_____
_____

Today, I'm grateful for

1. _____
2. _____
3. _____

Today I will explore a life that's *Rich With Purpose* by

_____
_____
_____
_____

Day 286

Beside every blade of grass there's an
angel whispering, 'Grow, grow, grow.'
– Kabbalistic saying

What thoughts and feelings does this quote inspire?

_____
_____
_____
_____

Today, I'm grateful for

1. _____
2. _____
3. _____

Today I will explore a life that's *Rich With Purpose* by

_____
_____
_____
_____

Day 287 • Weekly Check-in

What's come up for you this week around **Gratitude**?

_____

_____

_____

Have you noticed any changes in your financial life or in your connection to purpose? Have any synchronicities occurred?

_____

_____

_____

What does your Guru Within now recommend as the wisest path, both for your inner journey and for your action steps?

_____

_____

_____

Day 288

*Often it's because letting go is so fundamentally
simple that it seems enormously challenging.*
– Edward Vilga

What thoughts and feelings does this quote inspire?

_____
_____
_____
_____

Today, I'm grateful for

1. _____
2. _____
3. _____

Today I will explore a life that's *Rich With Purpose* by

_____
_____
_____
_____

Day 289

Unexpected travel suggestions are
dancing lessons from God.
– Kurt Vonnegut

What thoughts and feelings does this quote inspire?

_____

_____

_____

_____

Today, I'm grateful for

1. _____
2. _____
3. _____

Today I will explore a life that's *Rich With Purpose* by

_____

_____

_____

_____

Day 290

*The moment of surrender is not when
life is over. It's when it begins.*
– Marianne Williamson

What thoughts and feelings does this quote inspire?

_____
_____
_____
_____

Today, I'm grateful for

1. _____
2. _____
3. _____

Today I will explore a life that's *Rich With Purpose* by

_____
_____
_____
_____

Day 291

*One day you finally knew what
you had to do, and began...*
– Mary Oliver

What thoughts and feelings does this quote inspire?

_____

_____

_____

_____

Today, I'm grateful for

1. _____
2. _____
3. _____

Today I will explore a life that's *Rich With Purpose* by

_____

_____

_____

_____

Day 292

Growth demands a temporary
surrender of security.
– Gail Sheehy

What thoughts and feelings does this quote inspire?

_____
_____
_____
_____

Today, I'm grateful for

1. _____
2. _____
3. _____

Today I will explore a life that's *Rich With Purpose* by

_____
_____
_____
_____

Day 293

The robbers of time are the past and the future.
Man should bless the past, and forget it,
if it keeps him in bondage, and bless the
future, knowing it has in store for him
endless joys, but live fully in the now.
– Florence Scovel Shinn, The Game of Life and How to Play It

What thoughts and feelings does this quote inspire?

_____

_____

_____

_____

Today, I'm grateful for

1. _____
2. _____
3. _____

Today I will explore a life that's *Rich With Purpose* by

_____

_____

_____

_____

Day 294 • Weekly Check-in

What's come up for you this week around **Gratitude**?

_____

_____

_____

Have you noticed any changes in your financial life or in your connection to purpose? Have any synchronicities occurred?

_____

_____

_____

What does your Guru Within now recommend as the wisest path, both for your inner journey and for your action steps?

_____

_____

_____

Day 295

It's almost entirely our stories that determine whether we live in castles or prisons.
– Edward Vilga

What thoughts and feelings does this quote inspire?

_____

_____

_____

_____

Today, I'm grateful for

1. _____

2. _____

3. _____

Today I will explore a life that's *Rich With Purpose* by

_____

_____

_____

_____

Day 296

The creative process is a process
of surrender, not control.
– Julia Cameron

What thoughts and feelings does this quote inspire?

_____

_____

_____

_____

Today, I'm grateful for

1. _____

2. _____

3. _____

Today I will explore a life that's *Rich With Purpose* by

_____

_____

_____

_____

Day 297

The world isn't made up of atoms.
It's made up of stories.
– Muriel Rukeyser

What thoughts and feelings does this quote inspire?

_____
_____
_____
_____

Today, I'm grateful for

1. _____
2. _____
3. _____

Today I will explore a life that's *Rich With Purpose* by

_____
_____
_____
_____

Day 298

*If you feel stuck in your present life, if you feel no
enthusiasm for anything, if you think you have no purpose
or that you lost that purpose somewhere along the way,
I guarantee you are living in a dungeon made of stories.
And that none of those limiting stories are true.*
– Martha Beck

What thoughts and feelings does this quote inspire?

_____

_____

_____

_____

Today, I'm grateful for

1. _____

2. _____

3. _____

Today I will explore a life that's *Rich With Purpose* by

_____

_____

_____

_____

Day 299

You create your own reality.
There is no other rule.
– Seth, channeled by Jane Roberts

What thoughts and feelings does this quote inspire?

_____
_____
_____
_____

Today, I'm grateful for

1. _____
2. _____
3. _____

Today I will explore a life that's *Rich With Purpose* by

_____
_____
_____
_____

Day 300

*Tell me, what is it you plan to do with
your one wild and precious life?*
– Mary Oliver

What thoughts and feelings does this quote inspire?

_____
_____
_____
_____

Today, I'm grateful for

1. _____
2. _____
3. _____

Today I will explore a life that's *Rich With Purpose* by

_____
_____
_____
_____

Day 301 • Weekly Check-in

What's come up for you this week around **Gratitude**?

_____
_____
_____

Have you noticed any changes in your financial life or in your connection to purpose? Have any synchronicities occurred?

_____
_____
_____

What does your Guru Within now recommend as the wisest path, both for your inner journey and for your action steps?

_____
_____
_____

This month we explore...

Giving Back

What does the concept of **Giving Back** evoke for you?

_____
_____
_____
_____

Today, I'm grateful for

1. _____
2. _____
3. _____

Today I will explore a life that's _Rich With Purpose_ by

_____
_____
_____
_____

Day 302

Giving is powerful, transforming
both the giver and the receiver.
– Edward Vilga, *The Yoga of Money Manifesto*

What thoughts and feelings does this quote inspire?

_____
_____
_____
_____

Today, I'm grateful for

1. _____
2. _____
3. _____

Today I will explore a life that's *Rich With Purpose* by

_____
_____
_____
_____

Day 303

*If one desires to receive, one must first give.
This is called profound understanding.*
– Lao Tzu

What thoughts and feelings does this quote inspire?

_____
_____
_____
_____

Today, I'm grateful for

1. _____
2. _____
3. _____

Today I will explore a life that's *Rich With Purpose* by

_____
_____
_____
_____

Day 304

*You have not lived today until you have done
something for someone who can never repay you.*
– John Bunyan

What thoughts and feelings does this quote inspire?

_____
_____
_____
_____

Today, I'm grateful for

1. _____
2. _____
3. _____

Today I will explore a life that's *Rich With Purpose* by

_____
_____
_____
_____

Day 305

*We should give as we would receive, cheerfully,
quickly, and without hesitation; for there is no
grace in a benefit that sticks to the fingers.*
— Seneca

What thoughts and feelings does this quote inspire?

_____
_____
_____
_____

Today, I'm grateful for

1. _____
2. _____
3. _____

Today I will explore a life that's *Rich With Purpose* by

_____
_____
_____
_____

Day 306

That's what I consider true generosity:
You give your all and yet you always
feel as if it costs you nothing.
– Simone de Beauvoir

What thoughts and feelings does this quote inspire?

_____
_____
_____
_____

Today, I'm grateful for

1. _____
2. _____
3. _____

Today I will explore a life that's *Rich With Purpose* by

_____
_____
_____
_____

Day 307

You often say, 'I would give, but only to the deserving.' The trees in your orchard say not so, nor the flocks in your pasture. They give that they may live, for to withhold is to perish.
– Kahlil Gibran, *The Prophet*

What thoughts and feelings does this quote inspire?

_____

_____

_____

_____

Today, I'm grateful for

1. _____

2. _____

3. _____

Today I will explore a life that's *Rich With Purpose* by

_____

_____

_____

_____

Day 308 • Weekly Check-in

What's come up for you this week around **Giving Back**?

_____

_____

_____

Have you noticed any changes in your financial life or in your connection to purpose? Have any synchronicities occurred?

_____

_____

_____

What does your Guru Within now recommend as the wisest path, both for your inner journey and for your action steps?

_____

_____

_____

Day 309

Giving opens the way for receiving.
– Florence Shovel Shinn

What thoughts and feelings does this quote inspire?

_____
_____
_____
_____

Today, I'm grateful for

1. _____
2. _____
3. _____

Today I will explore a life that's *Rich With Purpose* by

_____
_____
_____
_____

Day 310

*Here's the catch: You have to act from this expansiveness
in your life as it is in order for things to change. The biblical
practice of tithing has power because it doesn't wait for the
future. It draws a state of flow into the present by insisting,
'In this moment, I have plenty. I'm rich enough to give.'
If even a dollar is the proper offering, it is enough.'*
– Tosha Silver, *Outrageous Openness*

What thoughts and feelings does this quote inspire?

_____

_____

_____

_____

Today, I'm grateful for

1. _____

2. _____

3. _____

Today I will explore a life that's *Rich With Purpose* by

_____

_____

_____

_____

Day 311

*If you can't feed a hundred
people, then just feed one.*
– Mother Teresa

What thoughts and feelings does this quote inspire?

_____
_____
_____
_____

Today, I'm grateful for

1. _____
2. _____
3. _____

Today I will explore a life that's *Rich With Purpose* by

_____
_____
_____
_____

Day 312

The Buddha said that no true spiritual life is possible without
a generous heart. Generosity allies itself with an inner feeling
of abundance—the feeling that we have enough to share.
– Sharon Salzberg

What thoughts and feelings does this quote inspire?

_____

_____

_____

_____

Today, I'm grateful for

1. _____
2. _____
3. _____

Today I will explore a life that's *Rich With Purpose* by

_____

_____

_____

_____

Day 313

I do not believe one can settle how much we ought to give.
I am afraid the only safe rule is to give more than we can spare.
– C.S. Lewis

What thoughts and feelings does this quote inspire?

_____
_____
_____
_____

Today, I'm grateful for

1. _____
2. _____
3. _____

Today I will explore a life that's *Rich With Purpose* by

_____
_____
_____
_____

Day 314

How wonderful that no one need wait a
single moment to improve the world.
– Anne Frank

What thoughts and feelings does this quote inspire?

_____

_____

_____

_____

Today, I'm grateful for

1. _____
2. _____
3. _____

Today I will explore a life that's *Rich With Purpose* by

_____

_____

_____

_____

Day 315 • Weekly Check-in

What's come up for you this week around **Giving Back**?

_____
_____
_____

Have you noticed any changes in your financial life or in your connection to purpose? Have any synchronicities occurred?

_____
_____
_____

What does your Guru Within now recommend as the wisest path, both for your inner journey and for your action steps?

_____
_____
_____

Day 316

What if we ourselves were the gift
we most want to receive?
– Edward Vilga

What thoughts and feelings does this quote inspire?

_____
_____
_____
_____

Today, I'm grateful for

1. _____
2. _____
3. _____

Today I will explore a life that's *Rich With Purpose* by

_____
_____
_____
_____

Day 317

Be a gift to everyone who enters your life, and to everyone whose life you enter. Be careful not to enter another's life if you cannot be a gift. (You can always be a gift, because you always are the gift—yet sometimes you don't let yourself know that.)
– Neale Donald Walsch, Conversations With God:
An Uncommon Dialogue, Vol. 2

What thoughts and feelings does this quote inspire?

_____
_____
_____
_____

Today, I'm grateful for

1. _____
2. _____
3. _____

Today I will explore a life that's *Rich With Purpose* by

_____
_____
_____
_____

Day 318

Money is but one venue for generosity.
Kindness is an even more valuable currency.
– Alan Cohen

What thoughts and feelings does this quote inspire?

_____
_____
_____
_____

Today, I'm grateful for

1. _____
2. _____
3. _____

Today I will explore a life that's *Rich With Purpose* by

_____
_____
_____
_____

Day 319

Attention is the rarest and purest
form of generosity.
– Simone Weil

What thoughts and feelings does this quote inspire?

_____
_____
_____
_____

Today, I'm grateful for

1. _____
2. _____
3. _____

Today I will explore a life that's *Rich With Purpose* by

_____
_____
_____
_____

Day 320

The greatest gift you ever give is your honest self.
– Fred Rogers

What thoughts and feelings does this quote inspire?

_____
_____
_____
_____

Today, I'm grateful for

1. _____
2. _____
3. _____

Today I will explore a life that's *Rich With Purpose* by

_____
_____
_____
_____

Day 321

*The best way to find yourself, is to lose
yourself in the service of others.*
– Mahatma Gandhi

What thoughts and feelings does this quote inspire?

_____
_____
_____
_____

Today, I'm grateful for

1. _____
2. _____
3. _____

Today I will explore a life that's *Rich With Purpose* by

_____
_____
_____
_____

Day 322 • Weekly Check-in

What's come up for you this week around **Giving Back**?

_____

_____

_____

Have you noticed any changes in your financial life or in your connection to purpose? Have any synchronicities occurred?

_____

_____

_____

What does your Guru Within now recommend as the wisest path, both for your inner journey and for your action steps?

_____

_____

_____

Day 323

*Generosity is an indispensable
part of our wealth journey.*
– Edward Vilga

What thoughts and feelings does this quote inspire?

_____
_____
_____
_____

Today, I'm grateful for

1. _____
2. _____
3. _____

Today I will explore a life that's *Rich With Purpose* by

_____
_____
_____
_____

Day 324

As we work to create light for others,
we naturally light our own way.
– Mary Anne Radmacher

What thoughts and feelings does this quote inspire?

_____
_____
_____
_____

Today, I'm grateful for

1. _____
2. _____
3. _____

Today I will explore a life that's *Rich With Purpose* by

_____
_____
_____
_____

Day 325

The value of a man resides in what he gives
and not in what he is capable of receiving.
– Albert Einstein

What thoughts and feelings does this quote inspire?

_____
_____
_____
_____

Today, I'm grateful for

1. _____
2. _____
3. _____

Today I will explore a life that's *Rich With Purpose* by

_____
_____
_____
_____

Day 326

*We make a living by what we get, but
we make a life by what we give.*
– Winston Churchill

What thoughts and feelings does this quote inspire?

_____
_____
_____
_____

Today, I'm grateful for

1. _____
2. _____
3. _____

Today I will explore a life that's *Rich With Purpose* by

_____
_____
_____
_____

Day 327

Generosity is the most natural outward expression of an inner attitude of compassion and lovingkindness.
– The Dalai Lama XIV

What thoughts and feelings does this quote inspire?

_____
_____
_____
_____

Today, I'm grateful for

1. _____
2. _____
3. _____

Today I will explore a life that's *Rich With Purpose* by

_____
_____
_____
_____

Day 328

*When you cease to make a
contribution, you begin to die.*
– Eleanor Roosevelt

What thoughts and feelings does this quote inspire?

_____

_____

_____

_____

Today, I'm grateful for

1. _____

2. _____

3. _____

Today I will explore a life that's *Rich With Purpose* by

_____

_____

_____

_____

Day 329 • Weekly Check-in

What's come up for you this week around **Giving Back**?

_____

_____

_____

Have you noticed any changes in your financial life or in your connection to purpose? Have any synchronicities occurred?

_____

_____

_____

What does your Guru Within now recommend as the wisest path, both for your inner journey and for your action steps?

_____

_____

_____

This month we explore...

Flow

What does the concept of **Flow** evoke for you?

_____
_____
_____
_____

Today, I'm grateful for

1. _____
2. _____
3. _____

Today I will explore a life that's _Rich With Purpose_ by

_____
_____
_____
_____

Day 330

*Raising your "Money Vibration" can really
help your financial situation, but sometimes
so can raising your credit limits.*
– Edward Vilga

What thoughts and feelings does this quote inspire?

_____

_____

_____

_____

Today, I'm grateful for

1. _____
2. _____
3. _____

Today I will explore a life that's *Rich With Purpose* by

_____

_____

_____

_____

Day 331

The definition of abundance is the ability to
what you need to do when you need to do it.
(Let go of the thinking that it has to be about money.)
– Darryl Anka, channeling Bashar

What thoughts and feelings does this quote inspire?

_____
_____
_____
_____

Today, I'm grateful for

1. _____
2. _____
3. _____

Today I will explore a life that's *Rich With Purpose* by

_____
_____
_____
_____

Day 332

*When you feel as though you are stuck in what you consider
to be lack, stop and take a deep breath. Then consider the
vast abundance of what surrounds you. The sky above, the
ground beneath you, the very magic that is in the air you
breathe. All of these things are yours already. Abundance
is simply the recognition of this, which is already in place
and constantly being added to, on and on, forever.*
– Frank Butterfield, *channeling The Communion of Light*

What thoughts and feelings does this quote inspire?

_____

_____

_____

_____

Today, I'm grateful for

1. _____

2. _____

3. _____

Today I will explore a life that's *Rich With Purpose* by

_____

_____

_____

_____

Day 333

How do you practice a feeling of abundance?
Just by picking something that feels good and
focusing upon it until it becomes more.
– Esther Hicks, *channeling Abraham*

What thoughts and feelings does this quote inspire?

_____
_____
_____
_____

Today, I'm grateful for

1. _____
2. _____
3. _____

Today I will explore a life that's *Rich With Purpose* by

_____
_____
_____
_____

Day 334

There are many expressions of abundance, not all of which are money. So as you focus on that which you are grateful for, you are tuning yourselves to the frequency of what has your attention. And anything that is of a similar vibration will begin to appear in your experience.
– Daniel Scranton

What thoughts and feelings does this quote inspire?

_____
_____
_____
_____

Today, I'm grateful for

1. _____
2. _____
3. _____

Today I will explore a life that's *Rich With Purpose* by

_____
_____
_____
_____

Day 335

*Quite deliberately you use your conscious mind playfully,
creating a game as children do, in which for a time you
completely ignore what seems to be in physical terms and
'pretend' that what you really want is real. If you are
poor, you purposely pretend that you have all you need
financially. Imagine how you will spend your money.*
– Jane Roberts, channeling Seth

What thoughts and feelings does this quote inspire?

_____
_____
_____
_____

Today, I'm grateful for

1. _____
2. _____
3. _____

Today I will explore a life that's *Rich With Purpose* by

_____
_____
_____
_____

Day 336 • Weekly Check-in

What's come up for you this week around **Flow**?

_____
_____
_____

Have you noticed any changes in your financial life or in your connection to purpose? Have any synchronicities occurred?

_____
_____
_____

What does your Guru Within now recommend as the wisest path, both for your inner journey and for your action steps?

_____
_____
_____

Day 337

When I was young I thought that money was the most
important thing in life; now that I am old I know that it is.
– Oscar Wilde

What thoughts and feelings does this quote inspire?

_____
_____
_____
_____

Today, I'm grateful for

1. _____
2. _____
3. _____

Today I will explore a life that's *Rich With Purpose* by

_____
_____
_____
_____

Day 338

Money isn't everything but it sure keeps
you in touch with your children.
– J. Paul Getty

What thoughts and feelings does this quote inspire?

_____
_____
_____
_____

Today, I'm grateful for

1. _____
2. _____
3. _____

Today I will explore a life that's *Rich With Purpose* by

_____
_____
_____
_____

Day 339

Money isn't the most important thing
in life, but it's reasonably close to
oxygen on the 'gotta have it' scale.
– Zig Ziglar

What thoughts and feelings does this quote inspire?

_____
_____
_____
_____

Today, I'm grateful for

1. _____
2. _____
3. _____

Today I will explore a life that's *Rich With Purpose* by

_____
_____
_____
_____

Day 340

Dogs have no money. Isn't that amazing?
They're broke their entire lives. But they get through.
You know why dogs have no money? ... No Pockets.
– Jerry Seinfeld

What thoughts and feelings does this quote inspire?

,_____
_____
_____
_____

Today, I'm grateful for

1. _____
2. _____
3. _____

Today I will explore a life that's *Rich With Purpose* by

_____
_____
_____
_____

Day 341

I learned in school that money isn't everything. It's happiness that counts. So momma sent me to a different school.
    – Zsa Zsa Gabor

What thoughts and feelings does this quote inspire?

_____
_____
_____
_____

Today, I'm grateful for

1. _____
2. _____
3. _____

Today I will explore a life that's *Rich With Purpose* by

_____
_____
_____
_____

Day 342

Once you have money, you can quite truthfully
affirm that money isn't everything.
– Louis Kronenberger

What thoughts and feelings does this quote inspire?

_____
_____
_____
_____

Today, I'm grateful for

1. _____
2. _____
3. _____

Today I will explore a life that's *Rich With Purpose* by

_____
_____
_____
_____

Day 343 • Weekly Check-in

What's come up for you this week around **Flow**?

_____

_____

_____

Have you noticed any changes in your financial life or in your
connection to purpose? Have any synchronicities occurred?

_____

_____

_____

What does your Guru Within now recommend as the wisest
path, both for your inner journey and for your action steps?

_____

_____

_____

Day 344

We shall not cease from exploration
And the end of all our exploring
Will be to arrive where we started
And know the place for the first time.
– T.S. Eliot

What thoughts and feelings does this quote inspire?

_____
_____
_____
_____

Today, I'm grateful for

1. _____
2. _____
3. _____

Today I will explore a life that's *Rich With Purpose* by

_____
_____
_____
_____

Day 345 • Final Check-in • Self Acceptance

What's shifted for you regarding **Self Acceptance** this past year?

_____

_____

_____

_____

_____

_____

_____

_____

_____

_____

_____

_____

_____

_____

_____

_____

_____

_____

_____

Day 346 • Final Check-in • Grounding

What's shifted for you regarding **Grounding** this past year?

_____
_____
_____
_____
_____
_____
_____
_____
_____
_____
_____
_____
_____
_____
_____
_____
_____
_____
_____
_____

Day 347 • Final Check-in • Balance

What's shifted for you regarding **Balance** this past year?

_____

_____

_____

_____

_____

_____

_____

_____

_____

_____

_____

_____

_____

_____

_____

_____

_____

_____

Day 348 • Final Check-in • Focus

What's shifted for you regarding **Focus** this past year?

_____
_____
_____
_____
_____
_____
_____
_____
_____
_____
_____
_____
_____
_____
_____
_____
_____
_____
_____
_____

Day 349 • Final Check-in • Support

What's shifted for you regarding **Support** this past year?

_____
_____
_____
_____
_____
_____
_____
_____
_____
_____
_____
_____
_____
_____
_____
_____
_____
_____
_____
_____

Day 350 • Final Check-in • Transformation

What's shifted for you regarding **Transformation** this past year?

_____
_____
_____
_____
_____
_____
_____
_____
_____
_____
_____
_____
_____
_____
_____
_____
_____
_____
_____
_____
_____

Day 351 • Final Check-in • Challenge

What's shifted for you regarding **Challenge** this past year?

_____
_____
_____
_____
_____
_____
_____
_____
_____
_____
_____
_____
_____
_____
_____
_____
_____
_____
_____
_____
_____
_____

Day 352 • Final Check-in • Adventure

What's shifted for you regarding **Adventure** this past year?

_____

_____

_____

_____

_____

_____

_____

_____

_____

_____

_____

_____

_____

_____

_____

_____

_____

_____

_____

Day 353 • Final Check-in • Gratitude

What's shifted for you regarding **Gratitude** this past year?

_____
_____
_____
_____
_____
_____
_____
_____
_____
_____
_____
_____
_____
_____
_____
_____
_____
_____
_____
_____

Day 354 • Final Check-in • Letting Go

What's shifted for you regarding **Letting Go** this past year?

_____
_____
_____
_____
_____
_____
_____
_____
_____
_____
_____
_____
_____
_____
_____
_____
_____
_____
_____
_____

Day 355 • Final Check-in • Giving Back

What's shifted for you regarding **Giving Back** this past year?

_____

_____

_____

_____

_____

_____

_____

_____

_____

_____

_____

_____

_____

_____

_____

_____

_____

_____

_____

_____

Day 356 • Final Check-in • Flow

What's shifted for you regarding **Flow** this past year?

_____
_____
_____
_____
_____
_____
_____
_____
_____
_____
_____
_____
_____
_____
_____
_____
_____
_____
_____
_____
_____

Day 357 • Looking Back

Life can only be understood backwards;
but it must be lived forwards.

– Søren Kierkegaard

What else has shifted, evolved or transformed for you this past year?

_____
_____
_____
_____
_____
_____
_____
_____
_____
_____
_____
_____
_____
_____
_____
_____
_____
_____
_____
_____

Day 358

Life is Flux.
– Heraclitus

What thoughts and feelings does this quote inspire?

_____
_____
_____
_____

Today, I'm grateful for

1. _____
2. _____
3. _____

Today I will explore a life that's *Rich With Purpose* by

_____
_____
_____
_____

Day 359

*Just lie back for a moment and contemplate
this wonderful, powerful Stream of Well-
Being, which moves unendingly in the
direction of your becoming, and toward
the fulfillment of that which is you.*
– Abraham-Hicks

What thoughts and feelings does this quote inspire?

_____
_____
_____
_____

Today, I'm grateful for

1. _____
2. _____
3. _____

Today I will explore a life that's *Rich With Purpose* by

_____
_____
_____
_____

Day 360

I am 100% certain that a Money Miracle is possible for you, but as we all know, Miracles usually resist our attempts to schedule them. Stay enthusiastic and committed, however, and they are sure to arrive at the perfect moment.
– Edward Vilga, *The Yoga of Money Manifesto*

What thoughts and feelings does this quote inspire?

_____
_____
_____
_____

Today, I'm grateful for

1. _____
2. _____
3. _____

Today I will explore a life that's *Rich With Purpose* by

_____
_____
_____
_____

Day 361 • Final Number Check-in

Please describe what's transformed for you regarding **Finances**?

_____

_____

_____

_____

_____

_____

_____

_____

_____

_____

_____

_____

_____

_____

_____

_____

_____

_____

_____

_____

Day 362 • Final Mindset Check-in

Please describe what's transformed for you regarding **Mindset**?

_____
_____
_____
_____
_____
_____
_____
_____
_____
_____
_____
_____
_____
_____
_____
_____
_____
_____
_____
_____
_____

363 • Final Body Wisdom Check-in

Please describe what's transformed for you regarding **Body Wisdom**?

_____

_____

_____

_____

_____

_____

_____

_____

_____

_____

_____

_____

_____

_____

_____

_____

_____

_____

_____

_____

Day 364

Sometimes what you think is an
end is only a beginning.
– Agatha Christie

What's come up for you this week around **Flow**?

_____

_____

_____

Have you noticed any changes in your financial life or in your
connection to purpose? Have any synchronicities occurred?

_____

_____

_____

What does your Guru Within now recommend as the wisest
path, both for your inner journey and for your action steps?

_____

_____

_____

Day 365

There's always more to learn, always more to explore
because your abundance journey is truly never-ending.
— Edward Vilga, *The Yoga of Money Manifesto*

What thoughts and feelings does this quote inspire?

_____

_____

_____

_____

Today, I'm grateful for

1. _____

2. _____

3. _____

Today I will explore a life that's *Rich With Purpose* by

_____

_____

_____

_____

Final Check-in

Can you summarize what has changed for you over the year on both practical and spiritual/emotional levels? How have you transformed…?

_____

_____

_____

_____

_____

_____

_____

_____

_____

_____

_____

_____

_____

_____

_____

_____

_____

_____

_____

Final Check-in

What new adventures of wealth and purpose do you see lying ahead?

_____

_____

_____

_____

_____

_____

_____

_____

_____

_____

_____

_____

_____

_____

_____

_____

_____

_____

_____

_____

Final Check-in

What else does your Guru Inner want you to know
about all the Abundance that lies ahead for you?

_____
_____
_____
_____
_____
_____
_____
_____
_____
_____
_____
_____
_____
_____
_____
_____
_____
_____
_____

AUTHOR BIO

Author Photo by Jonathan Pozniak

Edward Vilga offers nearly two decades of inspirational teaching experience connecting spirituality and wealth consciousness.

Besides creating the runaway bestselling course for DailyOM *A YEAR TO GET RICH WITH PURPOSE*, Edward is also the author of *The Yoga of Money Manifesto*. That book reached #1 on Amazon for all of New Thought.

Edward Vilga's other books include the novel *Downward Dog* and the bestselling *Yoga in Bed*. That book and DVD have been featured in *People* and Oprah's *O Magazine*, along with TV shows such as *Live with Kelly*, CBS' *Early Show*, and over 50 other publications. *Yoga In Bed* has been translated into over a dozen languages. The DVD has been downloaded and viewed over 1 million times.

Edward teaches in NYC and throughout the world. He is a Yale graduate. Most importantly, he is rarely seen without his chocolate lab, Belle.

You can follow his adventures––and enjoy free meditations, workshops, and books––at EdwardVilga.com